THE LIVES OF A BENGAL LANCER

F YEATS BROWN

THE LIVES OF A BENGAL LANCER

F YEATS BROWN

FRANCIS YEATS-BROWN

GYAN

Published by

GYAN

Gyan Publishing House
5, Ansari Road
Daryaganj, New Delhi-110002
Phone: 011-47034999, 9811692060
E-mail: books@gyanbooks.com

Distribution Network
gyanbooks.com
India, USA, Canada, UK, Australia

ISBN:978-93-7133-040-4 (PB)

First Published, 1930

2nd Impression 2025

Printed at: Gyan Press, Delhi.

THE LIVES OF A BENGAL LANCER F YEATS BROWN
Author Francis Yeats-Brown

BENGAL LANCER

BENGAL LANCER

by

F. YEATS-BROWN

1930

CONTENTS

CHAPTER I

NEW YEAR'S EVE, 1905

All the long way from Bareilly to Khushalgar on the Indus (the first stage of my journey to Bannu) I was alone in my railway carriage with two couchant lions.

Brownstone and Daisy were their names. Lord Brownstone, as he was entered in the register of the Indian Kennel Club, was the son of Jeffstone Monarch, and the grandson of Rodney Stone, the most famous bull-dog that ever lived. Brownstone was a light fawn dog, with black muzzle : I had bought him in Calcutta. His wife I had ordered from the Army and Navy Stores in England : she was a brindle bitch by Stormy Hope out of Nobby, with the stud name of Beckenham Kitty, but I called her Daisy. Both Brownstone and I were enchanted by her, for although rather froglike to an uninitiated eye, she fulfilled every canon of her breed's beauty.

When the train stopped, they stopped snoring. If anyone ventured to open the door, Daisy growled in a low, acid voice ; and Brownstone became a rampant instead of a couchant lion. So I remained, with leisure to reflect on this great, flat land we were traversing, and on my probationary year in it, just passed.

I was nineteen and a half. A year before I had become the trusty and well-beloved servant of His Majesty King Edward VII. Two months after receiving my commission I had sailed for India.

On the morning of my arrival at Bareilly an obsequious individual had waited on me with a bag of rupees. If I wanted money, he said, he would give me as much as I desired.

I wanted fourteen pounds at once, for an Afghan horse-dealer had brought to my tent door a five-year-old bay country-bred mare—a racy-looking Kathiawari, with black points, who cocked her curved ears engagingly and had the makings of a good light-weight polo-pony. I bought her on the spot.

I had only to shout *Quai Hai* to summon a slave, only to scrawl my initials on a *chit* in order to obtain a set of furniture, a felt carpet from Kashmir, brass ornaments from Moradabad, silver for pocket-money, a horse, champagne, cigars, anything I wanted. It was a jolly life, yet among these servants and *salaams* I had sometimes a sense of isolation, of being a caged white monkey in a Zoo whose patrons were this incredibly numerous beige race.

Riding through the densely packed bazaars of

Bareilly City on Judy, my mare, passing village temples, cantering across the magical plains that stretched away to the Himalayas, I shivered at the millions and immensities and secrecies of India. I liked to finish my day at the club, in a world whose limits were known and where people answered my beck. An incandescent lamp coughed its light over shrivelled grass and dusty shrubbery ; in its circle of illumination exiled heads were bent over English newspapers, their thoughts far away, but close to mine. Outside, people prayed and plotted and mated and died on a scale unimaginable and uncomfortable. We English were a caste. White overlords or white monkeys—it was all the same. The Brahmins made a circle within which they cooked their food. So did we. We were a caste : pariahs to them, princes in our own estimation.

It was pleasant enough to be a prince. Two dozen valets, and innumerable servants of other kinds had come, with testimonials wrapped up in blue handkerchiefs, to seek employment from me. The eagerness to be my valet had struck me as strange, for I did not then know that Indian servants like a young master, being human in his early years, and worth the trouble of breaking into Indian ways.

So it had come that I engaged Jagwant, a magnificent and faithful person, with elegant whiskers and an hereditary instinct for service. During the fifteen years that he was my friend and servant, I only once saw his equanimity disturbed ; and that was not by any worldly circumstance, but the powers of darkness. He was a Kahar, the highest caste of Hindu that will serve Europeans.

Jagwant was with me on board the train, in the servants' compartment adjoining mine. The remainder of my servants—a waiter, a washerman, a water-carrier, and sweeper, and two strong men for Judy (one to groom her and the other to give her grass)—I had paid off with a sense of relief. They had all smelt rather of snuff, and depressed me with their poverty and humility. Indeed, except for a *munshi*, who came daily to teach me Urdu, and the lordly Jagwant, I could not at this time feel any sympathy with the people of the country that was to be my home. I had expected and imagined much, but not this sad, all-pervasive squalor. Where were the colours and contrasts I had found in books ? Where were the Rajahs who ruled in splendour and those other Rajahs who drank potions of powdered pearls and woman's milk ? Where the priests and nautch-girls, and idols whose bellies held rubies as big as pigeons' eggs ? All I had seen was a tired people, mostly squatting on its heels and crouching over fires of cow-dung.

That, and my British regiment, was the India I knew. In the regiment, I had learned how to drill a company of riflemen, and to see that their boots and bedding and brushes were disposed in the manner approved by the Army Council, and that their hair was properly cut, and that they washed their feet. Also I had learned to hit a backhander under Judy's tail.

I had been rich during this last year (on the *chit* system) and had enjoyed myself enormously. My last act had been to sell Judy for double the price I had given for her, in order to settle my debts.

Now I was on my way north, to join the 17th Cavalry at Bannu, on the North-West Frontier.

The further we travelled, the larger and livelier the men looked. Women and children remained enigmatic bundles, small and inert.

Those doll-like babies with flies round their eyes—nineteen thousand of them were born every day in India. A staggering thought, all this begetting and birth. . . . And that girl with the very big brown eyes looking at me as if she was a deer, and I a hunting leopard, what was she thinking about? The bangles that glowed against her sunny skin? Her gods? Food? Why did some girls have a diamond in the left nostril?

Which of these people were Brahmins? Which Muhammedans? Which Animists? There were fourteen million Brahmins in India, I had read in a book, but to me the twice-born and the eaters of offal were alike. Did this slow brown tide that passed my carriage windows fight and make love like the quicker white? Did it possess parts and passions like myself? Perhaps I should find out, as a Bengal Lancer.

At Khushalgar, Jagwant and Brownstone and Daisy and I crossed the Indus and took another train to Kohat; and at Kohat, which we reached in the late afternoon, we packed ourselves into a tonga which already held an officer bound for Bannu, and his luggage.

Every moment of that eighty-mile drive had its thrill for me, but for my veteran companion the journey meant boredom and discomfort. He slept between the stages, waking up only when we changed ponies, in order to swear and drink sloe-gin.

Our ponies, galled at girth and neck, either jibbed backwards to within an inch of a precipice, or reared up like squealing unicorns and dashed downhill for a yard or two, then sat suddenly on their haunches, hoping perhaps that the harness would break and the tonga roll over them and end their wretched lives. Never once would they pull into their traces without some attempt at suicide. When suicide had been averted a rope was reeved under their fetlocks ; a groom pulled on the two ends, another pushed the tonga from behind, and the driver applied his whip scientifically to the ponies' ears. Cajoled and goaded, they would jump into their painful collars at last, and gallop on to the next halt.

On the road we passed men like Israelitish patriarchs, and tall, grim women in black, and a gang of Afridis who were dining on thick slices of unleavened bread and pieces of fat mutton. Stout fellows, these. The fire-light glinted in their hard eyes.

Once we slackened our pace while a boy ran beside us chattering about a tribal quarrel up the road. To help his cause, our driver agreed to carry twenty rounds of ammunition to the next stage : there we were waylaid by the opposing faction, who begged us to carry a hundred rounds for their party. My companion woke up at this moment and damned them all roundly, but agreed to take twenty rounds, this once, for he explained that we couldn't take sides.

At Lachi we encountered a band of beautiful young men with roses behind their ears. Where in all this waste, I asked myself, did flowers bloom ? As far as the forlorn hills of the horizon I could see nothing but rocks and pebbles.

On and on we rattled and crashed, until we came to the sugar-cane crops of the Bannu suburbs, with a mist over them, solemn and mysterious.

My companion loaded his revolver ; for there was a Garrison Order that we were always to be armed near cantonments, he told us. A fanatic had recently murdered our Brigade Major.

At the city walls stood a sentry with fixed bayonet. He opened a barbed wire gate for us, and we drove on to the house where my regiment and two battalions of the Frontier Force Infantry messed together. My companion descended here. I reported myself to the Adjutant of the 17th Cavalry and was shown to my quarters.

At dinner that night I sat between the Adjutant and an elderly Infantry Major. The latter breathed fumes of alcohol through his false teeth, like some fabulous dragon.

" Thank God I've finished with the frontier," he lisped. " Thirty years I've had of it. Now they've failed me for command. I'm retiring and be damned to them. There'th nothing but thtones and thniperth here. Up in Miramthhah the other day, a young Political Offither was thtabbed in his thleep by a Mathud recruit—thaid he'd noticed the thahib thlept with hith feet towards Mecca and that he couldn't allow thuch an inthult to hith religion. But they did a thing to the bathtard he didn't like. After he wath hung, they thewed him up in pigthkin tho that the *hourith* won't look at him in Paradithe. He'll have to anthwer the trumpet of the Archangel wrapped in the thkin of a thwine ! "

The port and madeira described constant ellipses over the long mess table, and the elderly Major helped himself at each round.

I questioned the Adjutant about *ghazis*. He told me that a certain Mullah of the Powindahs was preaching to the tribesmen from the fateful 5th verse of the 9th chapter of the Koran : " And when the sacred months are past, kill those who join other gods with God wherever ye shall find them ; and seize them and slay them and lay in wait for them with every kind of ambush." The murder of the Brigade Major had been a bad business. The *ghazi* hid in some crops at the roadside, waiting for the General, presumably, who was leading a new battalion into cantonments. The General had dropped behind for a moment, so the Brigade Major, who was riding at the head of the troops, received the load of buckshot intended for his chief. It hit him in the kidneys and killed him instantly. The *ghazi* tried to bolt, but was brought down wounded in the crops by a Sikh sergeant.

" Did they sew him up in pigskin ? " I enquired.

" Of course not," said the Adjutant. " That's a yarn. But we ought to do something about these murders. We're having a practice mobilisation the day after to-morrow, and may go out after raiders any day. There's a fair chance of seeing active service here, and decent shooting. Especially the snipe-jheels. The polo isn't up to much, but we mean to go in for the Indian Cavalry next year."

In the ante-room, the evening began to assume a festive mood. We dragged out a piano to the centre of the room. Well-trained servants appeared as if by magic to remove all breakable furniture (especially some tall china jars which had been taken by one of the regiments at the loot of Pekin) replacing it with a special set of chairs and tables made to smash. Senior officers bolted away to play bridge ; the rest of us, who were young in years, or heart, began to enjoy ourselves according to ancient custom.

Somebody found an enormous roll of webbing and swaddled up a fat gunner subaltern in it. A lamp fell with a crash. Wrestling matches began. A boy in the Punjaub Frontier Force brought in a little bazaar-pony and made it jump sofas. He had his trousers torn off.

I stood on my head in order to prove that it was possible to absorb liquid in that position. When this seemed tame, I dived over sofas and danced a jig with the elderly Major. Then a dozen of us went off to the billiard-room, where we played fives.

At midnight the fifty of us gathered in the ante-room again and sang " Auld Lang Syne," for it was New Year's Eve.

Hours afterwards, I left the dust and din and walked back under the stars to the bungalow in which I had been allotted a room. I was extraordinarily well pleased with myself and my new surroundings. Everyone in my regiment was the best fellow in the world—and that first impression of mine has not been altered by twenty years of intimacy.

As I sank to sleep, exhausted, I remembered that my feet were pointing westward, in the general direction of the Holy Ka'aba at Mecca, like those of the Political Officer in the Major's story, but I was too tired to move.

The New Year had begun very well indeed.

CHAPTER II

DURBAR AND A DOG FIGHT

Next morning the Adjutant took me to see the Commanding Officer. I was in uniform, belted and sworded and spurred, as I should have been had I been attending Orderly Room in a British regiment. The Colonel wore a brown sweater. His head was bent over a ledger, so that he did not see me salute. The Adjutant coughed. The Colonel looked up, then down to my toes, then up again.

My mind was a blank. He asked me if I was comfortable and I answered that I was extremely comfortable. There was a solemn pause during which all sorts of ridiculous things came into my mind, but I kept silence. Finally the Colonel said : " Well, don't let me detain you."

I withdrew in amazement and hesitated on the verandah, wondering what to do next, for the Adjutant had remained behind. There was a fierce-looking little Indian with a bright red beard sitting on the verandah smoking a cigarette. He looked me up and down, as the Colonel had done ; then jumped up and saluted, saying " Salaam, Sahib " in a high-pitched bark, and sat down again. He was in a uniform of sorts, wearing an old khaki jacket with the three stars of a Captain on the shoulder, but his legs were encased in Jodphur breeches and his feet in black slippers. I couldn't make him out at all. He kicked the slippers off, threw away the cigarette, and went into the Colonel's room without knocking.

"Who is the little red-bearded Captain?" I asked the Adjutant, who came out as this curious figure went in.

"That's Rissaldar Hamzullah Khan," he answered. "He's one of your troop commanders. You're posted to 'B' Squadron—all Pathans. As the Squadron Commander is away, Hamzullah will show you the ropes. He's a funny old chap; rose from the ranks. Come along with me now, and I'll introduce you to the other Indian officers."

We walked over to a tumble-down mud-hut, which was the Adjutant's office.

A group of big, bearded men sat there on a bench. They wore voluminous white robes and held walking-sticks between their knees. Another group, without walking-sticks, squatted. The squatters were called to attention by the senior N.C.O. The sitters rose, saluted the Adjutant and looked at me sternly. I was introduced and shook hands with Rissaldar Major Mahomed Amin Khan, Jamadar Hazrat Gul, Rissaldar Sultan Khan, Rissaldar Shams-ud-din and Woordie Major Rukan Din Khan—names that made my head reel. They all said "Salaam, Hazoor" (to which I answered "Salaam, Sahib") except one Indian Officer, who disconcerted me by saying "Janab 'Ali," which I afterwards discovered meant "Exalted Threshold of Serenity," or more literally, "High Doorstep."

In the course of these introductions, Hamzullah arrived. We shook hands. He eyed me narrowly, cackled with laughter and made a remark to the Adjutant in Pushtu—the language of the frontier.

The Adjutant translated :

"He wants to know if you can ride. He says you are the right build. And he says you are a *pei-makhe halak*—a milk-faced boy."

I felt anything but pleased.

"Hamzullah will take you round the squadron," said the Adjutant. "After stables, there's Durbar."

"If you will excuse me, Hazoor," said this surprising little man, as we walked towards "B" Squadron, "I will inspect the Quarter Guard, since I am Orderly Officer and it is on our way. Then we'll choose your chargers."

"I know exactly what I want as regards my horses, Rissaldar Sahib."

"Good. I will see that you get what you want."

Will you? I thought.

As we approached the guard, the sentry cried "Fall in!" in the queerest squeak. I lingered in the offing, to see how things were done in Indian Cavalry.

Five men and a sergeant sprang up from rope bedsteads and stood to arms. "Carrylanceadvance—visitingrounds" in one mouthful.

Hamzullah threw away his cigarette and stumped round, muttering comments in guttural Pushtu, which sounded like curses—and were.

When the guard was dismissed one of the men turned left instead of right. To my surprise, the sergeant took a stride towards him and struck him in the face. He was a huge yokel with long black hair heavily buttered. His turban fell off and unwound itself in the dust. Not a word was said. The man picked it up and joined his comrades. I stood rooted to the spot, expecting Hamzullah to place the sergeant under arrest.

He grunted and lit a cigarette. Perhaps, I thought, he had not seen.

Years later, when I became Adjutant, I learned what should be visible and what invisible in India *sillidar* cavalry. But until I had come to understand this, I was continually being surprised and sometimes shocked; therefore a small digression will be necessary if the reader is to see the Bengal Lancers as they were organised in those far-away years before the Great War.

Before the Mutiny, the yeomen and freebooters who served John Company brought their own horse and their own equipment to the regiment in which they elected to serve. They came ready to fight. They fought as long as there was loot to be had, and then returned to tend their crops.

Later, owing to the difficulty of maintaining a standard in equipment and horseflesh, it was found more convenient for the recruit to bring a sum in cash instead of a horse and saddle, but the principle remained the same, namely that the apprentice brought the tools of his trade.

In my day the cost of a *sillidar* cavalryman's complete equipment was about £55. If the recruit could not bring the whole amount, he brought at least £10, and owed the balance to the regiment, repaying the loan month by month out of his pay.

Each *sillidar* regiment (there were thirty, I think) maintained a *Chanda*, or Loan Fund, out of which these advances were made. As the administrator of this fund, the Commandant of an Indian Cavalry Regiment was to all intents and purposes the Managing Director of a company in which each man held from £10 to £55 of debenture stock, the debentures being secured on horses and equipment. The Colonel might also be considered as a contractor, who had engaged himself to supply the Indian Government with 625 cavalrymen, fed, mounted, provisioned, equipped (except for rifles and ammunition which were supplied by Government) at the cost of £2 per month per man, including all the transport and followers of the regiment—some 350 servants, 300 mules and nine camels.

The pay of the men was about 30 rupees a month—say £2—rising by small increases to £20 a month for the highest Indian rank, that of Rissaldar Major. At a very small cost, therefore, India was served by a body of yeomen complete with horses, tents, servants, mules, camels—an admirable bargain for Government, and a good one for its servants, for the *sillidar* cavalrymen was at once freer and more responsible than any other soldier in the Empire. He was freer, because men serving for the pittance they received after repayment of their loans had to be treated like the gentlemen adventurers that they were ; and more responsible because if a horse died or any loss to property occurred through negligence, the owner had to pay for it.

The regiment looked on itself as a family business. We bred horses as well as bought them. We all took an interest in our gear. The Colonel would no more have ordered a fresh consignment of saddlery without discussing the matter with his Indian Officers than a manager would install a new plant in his factory without consulting his directors. All this made for friendliness, and broad views. We had not time to make our men into machines. They remained yeomen who had enlisted for *izzat*—the untranslatable prestige of India.

That such a state of affairs should be abhorent to the mind of the War Office is readily understandable. The *sillidar* cavalry was abolished immediately after the

Great War on the plea that its mobilisation was complicated and unsatisfactory under such individualistic arrangements. So now our families are broken and scattered, and only a few ancestral voices, such as mine, remain to prophesy the woe that must attend their passing. But India rarely changes, and rarely forgets. When we give up trying to teach our grandmother to suck the eggs of Western militarism, she will again raise her levies in the way that suits her best.

To return to " B " Squadron. The Colonel came towards us, attended by the numerous staff that follows in the wake of every oriental autocrat. My Squadron Commander was away. What should I do?

Hamzullah's foxy eyes perceived my embarrassment. He whispered : " Blow your whistle, Sahib."

" I haven't got one."

" I'll blow mine."

The great man was upon us : Hamzullah blew a piercing blast.

" Go on with your work," said the Colonel, carrying a silver-headed malacca cane towards his helmet in answer to our salute. He wore civilian clothes.

What now? I turned again to Hamzullah, who barked, " *Hathe de lande*," which is Pushtu for " Hands underneath."

The men, who had been standing at attention with

elbows squared in front of their surprised horses, now resumed their brushing of bellies. The squadron kicked and squealed.

Stopping in front of a chestnut mare, the Colonel pointed at her fetlocks, which were hairy. Her owner dropped his brush, and rubbed them furiously, and the mare let fly with both heels, kicking over a bucket of dirty water.

"These devils never do what they're told," growled the Colonel. "Legs should have been done by now. Ask Hamzullah to tell you the Order of Grooming after I've gone. He won't see that it's carried out, but he'll tell you."

The procession continued, the Colonel leading, a dozen of us behind, hanging on his words.

"Tail wants pulling," he said to Hamzullah.

"Hazoor," said Hamzullah.

"A dirty horse is never fat."

"Hazoor," said Hamzullah.

"Staring coat. You must get rid of that boy if he can't keep his horse better. Fat enough before, under Khushal Khan."

"I shall warn him, Hazoor. He's a *zenana*-fed brat!"

"File his teeth," said the Colonel.

I started, but saw he was alluding to a raw-hipped waler.

"If that brute doesn't get fatter, put him down for casting."

"Yes, sir," said the Adjutant.

"When did I buy that mare?"

The Woordie Major produced an immense book, carried behind him by an orderly, and opened it at the proper place.

"Lyallpur Fair, 1903," mused the Colonel. "She's turning out well. I think we'll get a foal out of her. Send her to the Farm."

"Very good, sir," said the Adjutant, making a note of her number.

"And, by the way, give this young gentleman a copy of Standing Orders and Farm Orders."

"Another tail wants pulling," said the Colonel. "Do you know how to pull tails, Yeats-Brown?"

"Yes, sir."

"You had better get Hamzullah to show you how we do it here. Are the men for Persia chosen?"

"The ——?"

"Yes, Hazoor. I have chosen them," says Hamzullah.

"Bring them at Durbar with their horses. A great many tails want pulling."

When the Colonel came to the end of "B" Squadron I drew breath again. A blessed calm descended on us. Over in "C" Squadron the whistle sounded, and then the cry of "*Malish.*" Here we no longer bothered about grooming. The men stroked and patted their horses' backs, or leant against them for support. The East had returned to its old ways.

"Tell me, Rissaldar Sahib, about the Order of Grooming."

"Hazoor, it is in a book," answered Hamzullah in his high-pitched voice. "Five minutes for the horses' backs, ten for their blessed bellies, five for their foolish faces, and five for their dirty docks. A time to brush, and a time to rub, and a time to put everything in its place. That is good. But I am an old man, and cannot remember new ways. If I see a dirty horse in my troop, I beat its owner. If it is again dirty, I whip him with my tongue. And if that has no effect, he goes. Look at the result."

The result was that a hundred satiny coats shone in the sun.

"But some of the tails want pulling," I said.

"I have known the Colonel Sahib for thirty years," said Hamzullah, "and never yet have the tails of any troop been right. Not since we enlisted the first men and bought the first horses."

"Were you here when the regiment was raised?"

"Yes, Hazoor. I was a syce then, for I was too small and ugly to be a soldier. The Colonel Sahib was Adjutant. After five years he enlisted me as a fighting man. Before I die I shall be Rissaldar Major."

My heart warmed to him.

"I have much to learn, Rissaldar Sahib," I said. "I hope you will teach me."

"Men and horses are simple," he answered, "but mules are spawn of Satan. We can't get the syces for them nowadays. Wages are ridiculous. The young men all want to go to school. What do they learn there? Softness! Huh!"

We continued to stroll round the squadron, taking not the slightest notice of the men, some of whom were at work, while others kept dodging into their huts, where cooking was in progress. At last a trumpet call announced "Water and Feed," and after that "Durbar."

All India loves Durbars. They are her Parliaments, based on her ancient village system of a headman advised by a *panchayet*—five elders—and she may again rule herself by them.

An armchair is set for the Colonel, with a low table before it. By his side are stools for the Adjutant, Second-in-Command, the Rissaldar Major (senior Indian officer) and Woordie Major (Indian Adjutant). At right-angles to these high personages are two benches, on which the remaining British and Indian Officers sit in any order, intermingled. At the fourth side of the square, opposite the Commandant's table, are marshalled the persons to come before him.

All round, but particularly facing the Commandant, the men of the regiment are sitting or standing; spectators to our way of thinking, but something more in their own estimation, for they are there to see that justice is done. That they do not execute it themselves is immaterial; Durbar is a testing time for the Commandant. If he has not the wit and personality to rule, his deficiencies are soon apparent.

The Indian Officers rise, in turn, to present their recruits.

"A" and "B" Squadrons are bird-faced, white-skinned, keen-eyed boys, wild as hawks. They come from Independent Territory, and have called no man master. The Colonel looks them up and down, as he did me, and asks their parentage. Whether he accepts or rejects a candidate, his cold politeness remains unchanged: "He needn't wait," he says, or "Send him to the doctor," or "I don't think we've room," or "As he's a relation of yours, we'll give him a trial."

"C" and "D" Squadron recruits are Punjaub Muhammedans, slow and strong as the oxen they drive at the plough. They are darker than the Pathans, and have the manners of shrewd peasants, self-confident and a little suspicious. Then come the men for Persia (medalled veterans going to Teheran to serve as the Legation Guard) and the leave men. No soldiers in the world have so many holidays as Bengal Lancers. An Afridi wants to settle a blood feud. His uncle has been shot while gathering crops among his womenfolk. He must go at once to attend to the affair, or his face will be blackened in the village.

Then the defaulters. One of my men has allowed his horse to become rope-galled. A small offence apparently, but Hamzullah does not bring men before the Colonel unless he wants them severely dealt with.

" Fined fifteen rupees. You'll go, if you give us any more trouble," says the Colonel.

" Hazoor, I have a wife and three small children to support."

And indeed twenty shillings fine, to my thinking, comes heavy on a man whose pay is about five shillings a month after deductions.

" Your children are cared for by your brother," says the Colonel (who knows everything). " Get you gone."

Finally we come to the animals, who number a thousand and whose affairs are complex. Should the horses be fed on gram and barley, or gram alone? Should we buy ten truckloads of oats, or only one? Do the mules require an extra blanket on these winter nights? Engrossing questions these, and the Rissaldar Major and Hamzullah Khan and the Adjutant have much to say concerning them, for there is a nice distinction between discipline and administration in Durbar. Justice is a matter for one mind, economy for many.

Meanwhile, the junior British officer present at these proceedings sits twiddling his thumbs with boredom. He does not know that before the British came every ruler in India transacted business thus *coram publico*, and that to-day's meeting under the banyan tree is a continuance of that tradition. He does not know (or care) if our civil administration is becoming intolerably dull, and our justice dilatory. He does not know that Indians are becoming puzzled by our methods, and that the races of the North have buried a hundred thousand lethal weapons under their hearths in a determination never to be ruled by *babus*, brown or white.

Quotations from the Koran are being advanced in support of—what? The fit of a lance bucket? The quality of a picketing rope? Or is it something to do with the pay of syces?

Brownstone and Daisy have trotted up to see what their master is doing. They have no business here, but Brownstone, bolder than his mate, wriggles up to me, looking round the corner of his body and arching his back. He wants to be slapped on the loins. No Brownstone, this is a Durbar.

Daisy, looking very batrachian, is gazing up at me from a safe distance, her wizened muzzle cocked enquiringly. A chow, a terrier, and a friendly mongrel have also arrived, encouraged by some of the younger officers, who know that a dog fight has its uses.

"Take those brutes away," says the Colonel.

It is too late.

Chows are quarrelsome; this one growls and lifts his leg. Brownstone pounces without an ultimatum. The chow flicks round with a yelp and bites him on the ear. Brownstone's teeth close on his adversary's haunch; he had meant to strangle him, but missed. The mongrel dashes in to be at the death. In his eagerness, he collides with the terrier and they roll over and over together, snarling and snapping and writhing under the Colonel's table.

Daisy is skirmishing on the outskirts of the battle, I think, but it is difficult to see clearly in the cloud of dust and dog. The chow howls like a lost soul, and Brownstone, whom I have caught by the hind legs, looks at me with a red, pleased eye as if to say "I know you'll give me hell, but let me kill him first!"

The terrier is worrying my trousers, and Daisy has attacked a peculiarly tender part of the chow. I lift and pull and curse. For an instant Brownstone slackens his grip, but only to get a better hold, nearer the throat.

Someone has produced a pepper-pot. It is ground over Brownstone's nose, making him sigh. He won't stop killing for that. The Drill Major swathes the chow's head in a duster, to prevent him biting, and pulls one way while I pull the other.

"A bucket of water!"

It is sluiced over them ; we jerk, and jerk again. At last they come apart.

Daisy is kicked into a corner, hysterical with excitement. The mongrel runs away, and the chow stays put, licking his wounds gently. Brownstone is semi-conscious, but happy . . . I take him by the scruff of the neck and shake him ; a whip would be useless at such a moment.

So I have shoved my oar into the Durbar after all ! Is this the end of my career ?

Luckily, no irreparable damage has been done. Durbar was almost over. I follow the Colonel, who is walking back to his bungalow, attended by the Rissaldar Major, Woordie Major, Drill Major, Adjutant.

" Do you want me at the court-martial this afternoon, sir ? "

" No, you damned young fool. Why did you let that hell-hound off a lead ? Better take him to the horse-hospital."

" Very good, sir."

" By the way, have you chosen your chargers and orderly ? If not, then ask Hamzullah about them. You play polo, don't you ? There's a boy called Khushal in 'B' Squadron. I taught his father to ride, and he's a light weight who might do you well."

CHAPTER III

MASHEEN OF THE MIRRORED THUMBS

In the ivory box where my reels of memory are stored I can find only disjunct strips of film relating to my time at Bannu, for the heat has melted and distorted the sequence.

There is the night when the elderly Major shot himself by mistake ; there is the fascinating city of Peshawar, where I spent some months learning Pushtu ; there is the green polo ground at Bannu, and the rocky, desolate uplands where we learned our business of soldiering ; there is the daily round and its contrasting inner life. But there are only short strips of each, and a monotony of flapping *punkah*.

Khushal Khan, the orderly recommended by the Colonel, was a ringleted youth, with silky-curled moustache and manners as finished as his seat on a horse. He brought with him from the regimental store my equipment as a Bengal Lancer—a blue and gold full dress, with chain mail epaulettes ; a khaki coat of the same cut ; a blue and gold turban, and a khaki one ; a pair of large leather gauntlets, and two resplendent *cummerbunds*.

To tie a *cummerbund*, one end is held at full stretch by an assistant, while the wearer clasps the other on his hip and rolls himself into it. The *cummerbund* is six yards long, so it is impossible to practise such convolutions in a bungalow room. In my enthusiasm, I went out hatless into the courtyard with Khushal and during the few minutes that I stood there bareheaded, the sun worked my undoing.

Twenty-four hours later I could not longer have been called a milk-faced boy, for my complexion had become the tint of weak tea. I had sunstroke.

My brain buzzed with anxieties and urgencies that I could not allay. A frontier war was imminent, it seemed to me, and I must be ready for it, yet I could not collect my gear, for everything was in the wrong place, and my head too full to remember where anything might be.

The doctor came and prescribed bed and barley water. In two days I was up again, completely recovered. But in that short time I had learned that the sun is more than the giver of life. In England, Nature seems a tender mother, but East of Suez she changes her sex and she becomes Siva, Lord of Change and Destroyer of Names and Forms—Destroyer, that is, of ignorance.

The thermometer began to mount suddenly in March. For a time I enjoyed the heat, but as the relentless days wore on, life became a struggle with prickly-heat, brain-fever birds, sunstroke, dust, malaria.

We paraded for musketry at five o'clock in the morning and returned at nine, when a haze danced over the targets, and rifle barrels grew too hot to hold. Jagwant pulled me out of my boots ; I untied a necktie which had become a wet knot ; dressed in civilian clothes which soon hung pulpily ; breakfasted on glass after glass of milk and soda and ice-mango fool, until my body was swollen but my thirst not slaked. Afterwards I went to stables, attended office or Durbar, returned to my bungalow where various complicated accounts had to be written up and signed (for the *sillidar* system was already beginning to be smothered in red tape) and bicycled back to lunch in an air so hot that it caused men to muffle their mouths. In the afternoon, I attempted to read or answer letters or learn Hindustani, in a mist of sleep. At four o'clock I stirred up my senses with tea, put on long boots again, and rode down to polo.

For polo, Brownstone left his almost permanent place under the *punkah* and trotted out with his master. Daisy was going to have puppies and led a secluded life, but for Brownstone and me this was the best part of the day.

True, I leashed him directly we reached the ground, lest he should indulge in his own forms of sport, but he found all kinds of amusing smells there and I believe he enjoyed the games. His master was fighting and he would have liked to help. Once he tried to do so, by flying at the white throat of Milkmaid, my best pony but one, but he received a straight left from her forefoot which put him out of harm's way. After that, Khushal watched him.

My ponies were Crediton, a grand old chestnut who taught me tournament polo, and a glorious black Arab, who died of snake-bite on the muzzle before he was fully trained; Milkmaid, and my two chargers, Antinous and Ur of the Chaldees. These two carried me for three chukkers each, for, being bigger, I thought that they should do more work.

I made these good beasts sweat and suffer unnecessarily for my shortcomings, cutting their mouths and banging their fetlocks, but I fed them well and saw that they were decently groomed. If there be a heaven for horses, may they find peaceful paddocks there, and springier turf than that of Bannu.

After dinner, eaten still under the swish of fans, I went back to another *punkah*, by my bed and books.

My life was as sexless as any monk's at this time; and in a sense I was only half alive, lacking the companionship of women. But what is good for the Roman priest is good (I suppose) for the Indian Cavalry subaltern, who has work to do (like the priest) which he could scarcely perform if hampered by family ties. Certainly I possessed perceptions then which are uncapturable now in middle age. I was full of intuitions and enthusiasms, for when one sense is thwarted others are sometimes freed and quickened, although at what cost to the mind's rhythms I do not know. I do not know how far discipline of the sex life is a good thing. But I know that a normal sex life is more necessary in a hot than a cold country. The hysteria which seems to hang in the air of India is aggravated by severe continence of any kind; at the end of Ramzan, for instance, my fasting squadron used to become as lively as a basket of rattlesnakes. Many good brains in India have been bound like the feet of a mandarin's wife, so that they can only hobble ever after; and such cramping of the imagination may lose us the Empire.

Many times have I said that I would write these things. But now that I have done so, in this grey London weather, I cannot believe that I am not exaggerating. I cannot believe that it was too hot to bear a sheet on my skin, that I ingested six glasses of milk and soda for breakfast, had a malaria temperature twice a week for months on end, that my brain grew addled, and my liver enlarged, and my temper liable to rise like the fires of Stromboli. Yet so it was. Men's brains and bodies, like other machines, work differently at different temperatures; and India would be a happier country if we could always remember that, especially in Whitehall.

One night, when the temperature had risen

apoplectically (for a ceiling of thunderclouds had closed in on us) and I lay gasping on the roof of my quarters, a revolver shot rang out from a neighbouring bungalow. A moment before I had been drinking tepid soda water, and thinking of England, and cursing this stifling night through which the angel of sleep would not come. But now Providence had sent something better—raiders ?

Voices cried " *Halaka ghula di !* " (" 'Ware thief ! "). Khushal arrived with the first weapon to his hand, a lance.

I went out in my pyjamas to explore. Crossing the road in the direction of the shot, I found myself with a group of officers in the elderly Major's bungalow, where a curious story was related to me.

The elderly Major had been celebrating his approaching departure with more than enough champagne. On reaching his bed he had lain down quietly ; in a stupor, no doubt. Then his shattered nerves began to conjure up visions, and by the glimmer of the night-light which he always kept burning beside him, he saw a skinny outline at the foot of the bed. When he moved, it moved. Seizing a revolver in his trembling hand, he fired ; then he roared with pain, for he had shot not a face, but his own foot.

Next morning, he was hurried down to Kohat, with an orderly to put ice on his mangled toes and on his poor, deluded head. So he passed from our sight—

flotsam of the tide of Empire—and although this incident has been told before, I repeat it, since it really did happen to my elderly Major.

During this summer, cholera broke out in Bannu, of the sudden kind, that arches the victim backwards and kills people in a few hours. I do not know how many of the heathen it took in the bazaar, but it chose a dear old missionary lady from among the godly and the godless in cantonments. I was one of the officers deputed to carry her coffin to the little churchyard where lie the men of the Rifle Brigade who fell at Misar.

A British staff-sergeant was in charge of the proceedings. He was a stickler for formalities and he stopped our forlorn procession because we were carrying the departed head foremost. At the graveside he barked out the responses and twirled his waxed moustache so aggravatingly that I wished that the earth would swallow him.

I strolled back to the mess in an over-wrought mood, drank a quart of beer, fell asleep on a sofa. When I awoke, I looked differently on this earth.

The limit of life was darkness. God Himself was in the dark, else He could not have been so wicked as to create so much unwelcome death and unsatisfied desire. If God was good, why all this complicated begetting and hideous death in order to sustain a world which must in any case shrink and shrivel into nothingness? If God was kind, why this cholera?

I had been living in a smug mental sanctuary where unpleasantness was veiled in aphorisms. We all lived like that in England, where the seasons are beautiful. Here in High Asia we were closer to realities.

There was no God. I read Renan, and Anatole France's *Le Procurateur de Judée*, and a tract called *Roger's Reasons*, wherein Roger proves to his satisfaction that Noah took all the animals into the Ark. Then I sent for some missionary pamphlets which described various aspects of the religion of the Hindus, contrasting it with our own superior faith. Krishna had stolen the clothes of some milkmaids. Christ never did that. Kali was a goddess with a necklace of human skulls, dripping with blood. She danced on the body of her husband. Most improper. I was shocked, not by Hinduism, but by our missionaries who forgot the peccadilloes of Noah and the other patriarchs when comparing our sacred books with those of India.

Their unfairness inclined me towards Theosophy, and through Mrs. Besant I came to read about the System of the Vedanta. I find a faded note-book in which the following comments are entered, under the influence of an emotion that I cannot exactly recall:

" In the quiet hour of dawn, when the brain seems to be separate from the body and loth to return to the routine of dressing and the daily round, there comes to me a desire to rearrange my thoughts. I have a very miscellaneous lot of ideas. A good deal of rubbish has been acquired carelessly, and has stuck in my mind without any particular purpose. The treasures I have were gained in the moonlight, or seeing some hill-top struck by dawn. Always alone.

"Long before my teens I looked on clergymen as people endowed with more faith and hope than charity. I still hold to this. *Roger's Reasons* is a terrible book. There is no one so godless as a self-satisfied clergyman, for no one contradicts him." (I omit some lengthy immaturities here.)

"I have never doubted that I had a soul. But it is Mrs. Besant who has shown me the possibility of making this soul my own, and bringing it into my daily life and my eventual death. I have not been thinking about my soul much, but every time I look at her ideas, they seem to have grown more clearly in my mind.

"The Second Coming will take place in India. Only here can the descent of spirit into matter be understood. In the West we are rooted in convention, and gorged by too much print. The Churches are losing their hold on the young. Perhaps the Early Christians were happy, but now the West is sick with pain of its own begetting. It awaits a new interpretation of Christ in man.

"Life in India has not changed while Europe has been netting its land with rails, covering the sea with ships, sending messages over wire. Our feet have slipped in blood; and hers also have strayed into a tangle of abstractions and absurdities. But she is concerned with deeper and subtler things than self-government. In the wars which will come surely and soon we may learn to know each other better."

"In the wars that shall come surely and soon!" This was prophetic, if pompous. I was under the glamour of Mrs. Besant, of course, and it was she who first led me to explore the Aryan path.

The heat, much as I cursed it, saved me from a good deal of dreaming and the flail of everyday facts scourged out the introspective devils that lurk in the corners of the soul. I shut myself up in a darkened bungalow, alone with my thoughts and dogs, but, when I tried to write down what I felt, the pen slipped in my fingers, my hand made smudges on the paper, and the draught of the fan scattered my writings. The more I bathed the hotter I grew. The more I rubbed myself down, the wetter I became. So I was driven out of myself, into the sane world.

In November, too, squadron training began. "B" Squadron moved across the Kurram River, out of the hot-house atmosphere of Bannu to the open plain of Mamroz. For a delightful month we camped there. We were on the route by which Alexander invaded

India ; our tents between the rubble of two of his cities. Near one of them, while I was leading my troop, Ur of the Chaldees sank into a Bactrian room. But I had no time to think of Alexander ; one eye was on my Squadron Commander and the other on a V in the dark blue hills of the horizon.

Leading the men straight for long hours in the sun and dust—six hours in the saddle and never a minute between walls by day or night—wheeling and charging and cursing the rear rank—the rear rank is always cursed—and scouting and sketching and doing outpost schemes ; those days were amongst the happiest of my life. The men were brothers to us. After lunch we played Rugby football, or tossed the caber. Stables came at the end of the day. Then the horses were rugged up, watered, fed ; the sun sank in a blaze behind the Soleiman Dagh ; the tired squadron gathered round its tureens of mutton curry and flat-jacks ; and we three British officers went to splash in canvas baths.

The night air smelt very good when we emerged in our yellow fur-coats and Gilgit boots for dinner, and the crescent of Islam rode in a clear sky. Sometimes there was a bonfire and a Khuttuck dance ; more often we all went to sleep by nine o'clock, sated with exercise and meat.

From my bed I could see the squadron, and beyond it the jagged hills of Afghanistan, with Orion's Belt above them. I used to struggle hard to keep awake to enjoy the world a little longer. There was a white mule, a Houdini with his head rope, who was always loose : while I followed his movements, consciousness could not slip from me. I could see the mist from his nostrils as he stood looking at the sentries who passed and repassed the hurricane-lamp by the Quarter-Guard. Now he regarded me thoughtfully with the curious air of abstraction that animals assume at night. Now he was nosing under a tent-eave, where he had detected some sugar-cane. Now his long ears had caught the sound of footsteps, and he moved away to sip delicately at the water-bucket in front of the troop commander's tent. . . . And as I lay looking, and listening to the tent's flap, I travelled back into a past within me buried deeper than the Bactrian cities, and then forward suddenly : a miracle had occurred, it was already morning.

Réveillé rang out among the stones. My white mule led his kindred, who were already struggling out of camp with the syces to bring a day's fodder from cantonments. Horses stood dishevelled, with straw on their blankets, shivering. Men crept out of their tiny tents, clemmed with cold. Tea was brought to me, tasting of wood-smoke, and I drank it before I uncurled myself, slowly, luxuriously. For an officer, this camp life was glorious ; and even the men, who had not enough blankets to cover them, and slept two by two to keep warm, would not willingly have exchanged tents for houses.

When there are no such camps and no excuse to hunt and wander, what will this world be like?

One day I chased a hare, and that hunting brought a train of consequences, as a stone in water makes an enlarging circle of wave. It so happened that I was temporarily in command of the squadron, which had been left to me to take home quietly, doing a little drill on the way. When I saw this hare, however, I put spurs to my charger, for to pursue a flying thing was almost automatic. Besides, I wanted to test the pace of Ur of the Chaldees over five furlongs. Certainly I did not mean the squadron to follow me.

Afterwards, the trumpeter said I had given the order to gallop, but I imagine he mistook some unconscious movement of mine for a signal.

Whatever the reason, when I looked over my shoulder I saw the squadron following me in extended line, with outstretched lances. A ditch loomed up. I cleared it with a length to spare. Not so the squadron. Down went the horses' necks at the obstacle; some baulked, spilling their riders; half a dozen pecked, and rolled over on landing. Thoroughly disorganised now, the remainder poured after me in wild pursuit, madder than Rupert's cavaliers, and as bloodthirsty as those who followed the horned standards of Tamerlane.

Ahead was puss.

She made straight for camp, doubled back, tried to dodge between our ranks. A chance hoof broke her back.

A couple of raw country-breds, just out of training-school, had run away with their riders. Out of all control, they dashed straight among the tents, falling there amidst a whinnying of tethered horses.

The squadron leader came out in his shirt-sleeves, biting at his cheroot. I had reined up in a muck of sweat, and felt foolish, sitting there on Ur, amongst my delighted men, with a small brown thing at my feet, kicking convulsively.

A sowar dismounted and opened his jack-knife.

" Kill it quickly," I said, for the hare was working its hind legs as if it still hoped to escape.

The youth looked up in surprise.

" I'm not sure if the meat is lawful," he said, " but I will kill it lawfully." And with a muttered " *Al hamd 'ul 'illah,*" he cut her throat.

" What the hell——" said the squadron leader.

My explanation sounded thin. However, we had the hare jugged for dinner that night.

Over our madeira, the squadron leader and I discussed the necessity for speaking to the Pathan in his own language.

" Urdu won't do," said my Major, " you must know Pushtu if you want to command these blighters."

Now to learn Pushtu I should go to Peshawar, the

metropolis of the Pathans ; and I pointed this out. The squadron commander agreed, and it was thus, thanks indirectly to the hare, that I found myself in that city at the end of Squadron Training.

I learned more than the knowledge required to pass the Higher Standard examination in Pushtu while I lived in Peshawar.

If you visit its bazaars by day, when roses are sold in the streets and proud fathers carry their babies shoulder-high, you will see one thing. By night, when the city gates are shut you will see quite another and more intimate side of the Pathan.

Countries, like people, are loved for their failings. I began to love this frontier land. But my eagerness to look into the Central Asian heart had a purpose other than that which I acknowledged even to myself. To pass the Higher Standard was a reasonable ambition, but what I really required for my happiness was to get out of the rut of soldiering. My life had been cramped into a conventional mould. Now I was beginning to shake myself free.

Western civilisation had bullied and bored me. The floods of tears I had shed over Latin syntax, my hysterical inability to construe, my short sight (which kept me back at games) and an emotional crisis which blighted my life at the age of sixteen, had left scars and sullennesses. I had not been a success at school. Nor did I like Sandhurst, except for the cavalry camp at the end of my time there. Drill disgusted me. I was hopeless at cricket and too slow for football. Here in India I was finding myself.

The nautch-girls of Peshawar, I had been told, were of a beauty to make the dog-stars weep. Their bodies were cypresses, their teeth camomile petals, their eyes falcons of morning, their lips like Solomon's seal. I went to visit their houses, therefore, in expectancy.

My Pathan friend and I were dressed in gold-laced waistcoats and jet black turbans with gold fringes; we wore roses behind our ears; our eyes were painted with collyrium; we carried daggers, and my friend a favourite fighting quail in a small gilt cage. We visited the caravanserais of the Dabgari quarter which are hotbeds of Central Asian intrigue and vice. We fought quails and played *andhabazi*, the great egg game. It was an amusing world.

I learned to smoke hashish, whose local name is *charas*. I heard stories of Lughman Hakim and Iskunder and Aflatoon that were told long ago in Baghdad by other Scheherezades. Sometimes I understood these tales and blushed under my walnut-oil complexion; more often I lost the thread, but still listened, letting the accents and idioms of the narrator sink into my mind.

My friend told the company that I was a Kashmiri, but I doubt whether they believed that. The women asked no questions, however, for our rupees were as good as any others ; their business was not to discuss the antecedents of their visitors, but to amuse them : like the *hetairai* of the Athens of Pericles, they were hostesses as well as courtesans.

I fell in love with a famous dancer—Masheen by name. Her fee was sometimes as much as a thousand rupees for a single night—rich men gave her that, not milk-faced boys. Her thumbs were adorned with mirrors. She had mesmeric arms and wrists. Her whole body, from neck to ankles, was aflash with bracelets and rings, and on her bare stomach one emerald shone. She was leisurely in her movements, a mistress of time as well as her muscles, beginning always with her finger tips to slow cadences, and continuing with hands and arms and shoulders until the wave passed into her flexible body. Then that too seemed to melt entirely into the rhythm of the drums, which had now grown wild and quick. She seemed no longer human, but sound itself : her voluminous skirts became the tapping of the *dol*[1] and her henna-ed hands the fluting of the *serenai*.[2] She was more than her dancing, having transcended personality by merging with the voices of Creation.

Cross-legged, chewing betel-nut, and occasionally

[1] Drum. [2] Flute.

taking a pull at a *charas*-laden hookah, I watched her first with curiosity, then fascination. Here was release and rapture. As she danced on and on to the music of her drunken drummers, some rhythm or religion from the night of time sounded on my skin and gathered itself into my pulses. I could feel as well as hear the beating of the drums.

The smell of crushed geraniums brings back the memory of these Peshawar nights. The *charas* I smoked made me sometimes imagine that I could crawl through keyholes, and sometimes that I could step over the Himalayas, but if it harmed my body at all, it shed a countervailing blessing on my spirit, for by its aid I could always return to the ecstasies and entrancements of the nautch.

Those infinitely subtle movements slid into my soul and spoke to me of times long past, when the rhythms of the body were worshipped in the pantomime of Creation, and David danced before the altar of Jehovah. Somewhere in space these spells survive, for their delight is deathless. " He who is intoxicated with wine will be sober by dawn, but he who has lost his senses to the Cup-bearer will not recover until the Day of Judgment."

CHAPTER IV

THE DELHI ROAD

The day that I heard that I had passed the Higher Standard Examination in Pushtu with credit, orders also came that the regiment was to march south, and not only south, but to my old cantonment of Bareilly. Moreover, eight beautiful babies were born to Daisy.

We were to march for three months, down half India, through the Punjaub and on to the United Provinces, where we would find pig and deer and panther, and lakes over which wild duck wheel, and old thatched bungalows under the shade of mango trees. In Bareilly, new doors would open to my knocking.

On the last night at Bannu our men gave a display of tent-pegging by torchlight. They rode down singly first, galloping at a line of pegs soaked in kerosene oil ; and each peg came up in a whirl of fire.

Their cry was "*Ali, Ali, Ali—Yi-hai !*" ("Ali—I have it !") One of these paladins invoked the Name of the Lord of the Worlds, King on the Day of Judgment :

Bismillah hir-rahman nir-rahim—
Al-hamdul-illah rabi lalamin—
Ar-rahman nir-rahim
Malik-i-yumi din. Yi-hai—YI-HAI !

It was a fierce prayer, gabbled as he galloped at the peg. He flamed past us with eyeballs and teeth glinting, and could not stop his horse, so that he rode the whole circuit of the field, twirling his lance and roaring with open throat upon the name of Allah. Then came sections of four—Afridis and Khuttucks and Tiwanas and Khalils—thundering out of the dark in their flowing white robes. I was proud of the regiment !

Next morning, we trotted away in a long column of dust, with the sunlight glinting on our lances through the kikr trees of the Kohat road :

And I said, I will 'list for a Lancer
O who would not sleep with the brave !

For three months we marched, past Rawalpindi, Ferozepore, Ludhiana, Rurki, and Lahore, moving faster, so the Colonel said, than the horsemen of Alexander pursuing Darius. The quick spring of India ended all the quicker for our southward march. The weather grew hot, and our hearts light, for each day brought us nearer the Ganges with its river grass and bamboo thickets, where the heavy boar wallow.

At Lahore, a strange thing happened in the gardens of Shahdara. I went to visit Jehangir's tomb there, with a friend and his bull terrier. This dog came with us to the garden, but we tied her up before entering the tomb, out of respect for a Moslem burial-place.

She whined and yelped, so when we were going up to the roof we asked the resident Imam whether there would be any objection to her following us ? The Imam shrugged his shoulders, and said that he had no objection at all, but that he advised us to be careful. My friend loosed her, and she came rejoicing. Another visitor with a dog took his also up to the roof.

Now the wide flat top of Jehangir's tomb is bounded by a parapet. My friend's bitch hunted about for a moment or two, with her nose down, as if she were following a scent. Then she jumped over the parapet, and was dashed to pieces on the path below. It happened so quickly there was no time to call her. We ran down and picked her up while she was still breathing, but every bone of her poor body was broken, and she died before we could take her to a vet.

We did not go back to the place of tragedy, but next day we heard that the other man's dog had done exactly the same thing a few minutes afterwards. Both animals committed suicide. I can vouch for the facts, but have no explanation to offer, except that conceivably the dogs saw something that we did not.

Dilli dur ast.

It is a far cry from Lahore to Delhi, but thither we

must go at a stride, lest this story grow too long in the telling.

While we were entertaining some friends in our mess tent at Delhi, a sacred bull strolled through the camp with such a cocksure air that I was tempted to make a bet that I would ride it. It tossed me tent-high, however, then tripped itself over a rope and fell sprawling, outraged, amazed. This was too much for Brownstone, who had been watching the proceedings from his bath-tub kennel : he squirmed out of his collar and pounced on the throat of his hereditary enemy. How I pulled him off I cannot now remember, but by the time I had succeeded in doing so a considerable crowd had collected, for we were in the very middle of Delhi, opposite the Juma Masjid mosque.

Here was an insult to the Hindu religion offered by a brutal soldiery. I had an awkward interview with the Colonel next day, and a pleasanter one with the plaintiff Hindus, for I was so anxious to stand well in their estimation that I would willingly have given them a sacred bull a-piece, instead of the small contribution for the Sick Animals' Dispensary which they demanded by way of compensation ; and it was therefore in a very favourable atmosphere that I was able to put a question that I had long wanted to ask.

" A *guru*, Sahib ? " answered the Brahmin whom I had addressed, " you can find one in Benares if you go there."

" Benares is a long way," I said. " Surely there are *gurus* in the capital of India ? You yourself, for instance, could tell me of Yoga."

" Sahib, you are a soldier, and the *karma* of blood is blood. You must choose between two paths. As it is written, 'If you are in the world, be rightly of it.' When you are old as I, it will be time enough to turn to contemplation of things of the mind."

" I don't see why I shouldn't be a Yogi as well as a soldier ! "

" Perhaps you could be both in your own country," the Brahmin answered, " but not here. In India we live in invisible cages."

" Invisible cages—— ? "

" Caste. But we have no industrial system, nor do we condemn our girls to the sterility which you consider natural if they do not succeed in the competition for husbands. We recognise the right of every human being to a mate. Yet the fetters we have forged through caste are dragging us down—to the level of Western civilisation."

"We have nothing like your child marriage, *pandit-ji*."

" You make your children work when they should be playing," he answered quickly. "Besides, many of us disapprove of child marriage, but customs that have grown up through centuries cannot be abolished in a day. Even in England the age of consent is still fourteen."

"I agree with you, *pandit-ji*, that we are far from perfect. I love my country in spite of her faults. But I admit them. I have long felt that Western civilisation is sick. That is why I want to learn about Yoga. If I did, would I be suspected of being a spy?"

"No. Your own people might think you mad; but we would not think you a spy. There are no secrets to be discovered in Yoga, but there are many things to be learned. Yoga is not a medicine to take at a gulp. Nor is it a dogma. It is a set of exercises. You begin at the beginning and go on steadily, for until the first exercise is mastered the second cannot be understood. The same is true of the integral calculus. But there is this difference—Yoga is a physical as well as mental process. It is written that just as the sweetness of molasses can only be realised by the tongue and can never be explained by thousands of words, so Yoga can be realised only by the senses and never explained by words. You come from a culture that has made a fetish of the brain. You come from a different climate. You are young, confident that you have only to say a thing and it is. In India things are never what they seem. We are an old race, and our religions—for they are many—are full of beauty and decay."

The spate of words stopped suddenly.

"I want to learn of their beauty," I said.

"Beware of it, I warn you. But if you are serious, Sahib, I will tell you of the first step in Yoga. It consists in the cultivation of the qualities of forbearance towards all life created, courage, secrecy, concentration, faith, honesty, self-control, cleanliness, cheerfulness, perseverance and purity.

" And humility," he added, as if it was an afterthought. " Humility is indeed very necessary. Some of the *gurus* make their disciples sweep out the latrines of the untouchables with their hair. I have a nephew at Agra who is doing some such thing."

" Where could I find him ? " I asked.

" I do not know exactly. At a burning-*ghat* probably. His name is Sivanand Joshi. But I advise you to have nothing to do with Yoga. You Englishmen are practical about material things. Be practical about mysticism also. Build your Rome brick by brick."

" I have no straw for the bricks of my mind, *pandit-ji*."

" When you are ready to build, Hazoor, you will find the straw. It always happens so."

CHAPTER V

THE KING COBRA AND THE HERALD OF THE STAR

Chance seemed to guide my feet towards the sages of the Ganges, and animals. The hare had awakened in me the ache for *ahimsa*.[1] Then a bull had helped me on the road to Benares. Next, a king cobra uncoiled itself as a portent of the things that lay about me, unseen. But the veils of *maya*[2] cannot be pierced save through experience. They twitched aside, then closed again.

The cobra came one afternoon in early spring when I was installed in my bungalow at Bareilly. I was studying maps of the district at the moment, considering how best we should plan our camps during the coming pig-sticking season ; when unexpectedly—for it was the hour for repose—Jagwant appeared. He salaamed, and said that a man had been bitten by a snake.

" What man ? " I asked.

" Just a man, Cherisher of the Poor," said Jagwant. " He is going to die in the road outside our house."

I ran out to my bungalow gate, and found there a group of syces and grasscutters gazing apathetically at a prostrate figure.

[1] Non-violence towards all created things.
[2] Name, form, time, space and causation.

Evidently the man was a grasscutter who had been scraping up the sweet *dhub* grass by the roadside, for his implement was beside him and his loin-cloth was half-filled with fodder. A passing postman had seen him and had told Jagwant. Jagwant had gone to look, and had decided that he could do nothing personally, for the man was of low caste.

His lips were already blue when we carried him into the verandah. I scribbled a line to the regimental doctor and sent Jagwant off with it, telling him to return with some brandy (there was no pollution for him in that). Then I searched for the mark of a wound on the grasscutters's scaly legs and gnarled hands, but could find none.

When the doctor came he found two livid spots on the palm near the thumb, about half an inch apart, but it was too late to incise them. The man was dead.

"I know a *saddhu* who can bring even the dead to life," said a native hospital assistant as soon as his chief had gone.

At my request, he hurried off to the bazaar, and returned about an hour later with the *saddhu*, who proved to be an emaciated, ash-smeared creature with matted hair, carrying a begging bowl and a flute.

Immediately, without a word to me, the *saddhu* seated himself a-straddle on the corpse, parted its lips, breathed into them, and began a sing-song *mantra*, trembling violently.

"Your Honour," said Jagwant, who had observed those proceedings gloomily, "I shall have to pay money to the Brahmins if he brings the spirit back. This is magic of the left-hand path."

But the *saddhu* sat back with a sigh, took a pinch of snuff from a fold of his loin-cloth, and said:

"I can animate the body for a few minutes to-night, Sahib, if you will send it to some lonely place, but it is too old and weak and full of poison to live. The Great One that killed this man is probably in your Honour's house, or near it, and I can of course make it come out of its hiding-place."

"You shall have ten rupees if you can find the snake," I said: "but how shall I know that it is the same snake?"

"I will show you the Prince," answered the *saddhu* confidently, "I have done the same thing for the *Burra Lat Sahib* [the then Lieutenant-Governor] and other *Burra Sahibs*."

As he entered my room, Brownstone rose and stretched himself, sleepy and calm and friendly, but instead of his usual polite sniff at a guest, the hairs on his back rose like hackles on a cock. He waddled away with stiff legs and limp tail.

The *saddhu* peered and poked about my room. Finally he said: "The Prince is in this house," and sat down on the floor, with his reed pipe.

I took a chair, feeling rather excited, for no sound

came from the *saddhu's* instrument, although he was playing it. It was strange to think that the snake might be already keeping time to the reed, waving and weaving invisibly to this inaudible music.

After some ten minutes, Jagwant ushered in a waiter, carrying my afternoon tea. Brownstone came to sit by me, on the side away from the *saddhu*, and gazed at the buttered toast with such intensity that icicles of saliva formed at his chops.

" The Prince is there," said the *saddhu*, pointing to a box near the bathroom door.

I went over and pulled it out from the wall, but nothing stirred. The squeak of Daisy's puppies came to us from an adjoining room, and the *saddhu* laid his reed down.

" There are too many dogs in this house," he said. " My Lord is distracted. Will your Honour send them away ? "

I told Jagwant to remove Brownstone and that Daisy and her children must be taken to the sweeper's house.

" I can give you another fifteen minutes," I said, " while I change for polo."

" He will come at once now, Hazoor," he answered, mopping his forehead. " My Lord has been very close all the time."

Trickles of sweat ran along his ashy ribs and he was trembling again, as when he had sat on the corpse. He played, and I could just hear him now. For a minute he continued, then he rose and urged me with a motion of his whole body towards the bathroom door.

Under the bulge of the tin bath a shadow lay. I went closer, thinking it would vanish. Instead, it uncoiled itself like a whip-lash. For a moment I feared that the cold at the pit of my stomach would paralyse my arm, but when the cobra hissed up on to its tail, with hood outspread, I hit out with the walking-stick I carried, and fear vanished. I struck at it two or three times. It was a hamadryad.

The *saddhu* piped loudly, and rolled his eyes, inspiring me with an unreasonable but instinctive revulsion.

" Hut ! *Hut ! Hut !* " said Jagwant, waving him away.

That was hardly fair.

"What is the matter with you, Jagwant ? " I said. " I want to talk to this man who has saved us all from being bitten—and you hustle him out of the house."

" Hazoor, the man is a Tantrik. What does your Honour want with a beef-eating magician ? "

" That's my business."

When I paid the *saddhu*, not ten, but sixteen rupees, I told him that I would give him yet another gold *mohur* if he would tell me how he brought the snake.

He laughed at that.

" I can teach you a first-class card trick, Hazoor."

" I don't want tricks. How did the cobra come to be in my bathroom ? "

" It came, Hazoor. That is all I know. If you send it

to the hospital, the Doctor Sahib will tell you that its fangs are empty. It killed the grasscutter."

"How do you know?"

Again the *saddhu* laughed.

"I know there is a cat in your roof," he said.

That was probable. Polecats lived in many of these old thatched bungalows, and there was the stain of one on my cloth ceiling. He would answer none of my questions.

"My eyes are sharp," was all he would say. "So sharp that they go through walls."

"Can I acquire your knowledge?" I demanded again.

"What does a great Sahib like your Honour want with such things? I learnt from my father and my father learnt from my grandfather. My father could pour water into his mouth and pass it directly through his bowels. My grandfather was waxed all over and buried alive for forty-three days. I can swallow five different coloured handkerchiefs and vomit them up in any order you wish, and I can lift a cannon-ball with my eyelids. If your Honour wishes to see these things, I can come again, but my *ekka* is waiting to take me into the city, where I have an appointment. Salaam, Hazoor!"

After polo, I questioned Jagwant on the subject of Tantriks. He told me that some of them were wise and good men, but generally difficult to deal with. It was best to avoid Tantriks. Some of them ate dead bodies. Others ate beef. Others could transport themselves to the Himalayas in the twinkling of an eye and talk with tigers as friend to friend. One of their habits was to haunt the burning-*ghats*, where they would put rice and *ghi* between the teeth of a corpse—preferably that of a woman who had died in child-birth—and summon a spirit into it, so that it sat upright and spoke. When this happened there was a bugling of ghostly conches and a rattle of unearthly drums, very terrible to hear.

I demanded that I should be introduced to someone who was an expert in these matters. As usual Jagwant salaamed.

Soon afterwards a Brahmin friend of his appeared—an overseer holding a position in the Public Works Department—who unlaced his boots and left them in my verandah before entering, although I begged him not to do so.

" In Benares you will find real *gurus*," he said, accepting one of my cigarettes and speaking in fluent English. " There are thousands of teachers there of an unquestionable perspicacity and skill, sir, who would look with disdain upon the art of charming cobras."

" Have you heard of Mrs. Besant ? " I asked.

" Of course ! A great and good woman. She is truly a mother to my unfortunate country."

We discussed Theosophy for some time and finding

that he knew nothing about it, I tried to steer the conversation towards the Tantriks.

The pundit looked shocked. He had never heard of dead men being raised. There was a *saddhu* at Puri who claimed to be able to resurrect sparrows that had been wrangled by breathing *prana*[1] into them, but it was possible that he was an impostor. He did not believe such things. When he had taken his B.A. degree he had studied comparative religion and had come to the conclusion that all the great faiths of the world were true, and none of them completely satisfying.

" Do you believe in God, *pandit-ji* ? " I asked.

" Oh, no ! Not a personal God," he answered. " Such vulgar ideas are only for uneducated men."

The pundit would tell me nothing about his philosophy. We were polite to each other, but there was a barrier between us that nothing but time or violence could have lifted. I afterwards discovered he was no mean Vedanta scholar and could have said more in half an hour than I could have assimilated in a month. But I had not remembered a very simple thing : in the East information is not to be had for the asking. The Brahmins consider knowledge to be a dangerous tool, and the giving of it to the ignorant like giving a razor instead of a rattle to a baby.

We Europeans are always giving something to somebody. Christianity, for instance. Then education. Now

[1] Vital force.

we give our ideas of democracy. All this is alien to the Hindu mind which has outgrown the culture which inspired that revealing hymn :

Can we, whose souls are lighted
With wisdom from on high,
Can we to men benighted
The lamp of light deny ?

The high-caste Hindu is arrogant enough in his own way (coming as he does from the same stock as ourselves) but he is convinced that no illumination can be given to minds that do not wish for it ; that no outer theory can make men free ; that no medicine will work while the patient sleeps, except to the patient's ruin.

These differences go deep down. We can bridge them with our brains, but hardly with our hearts. The best we can do, on either side, is to avoid arrogance.

Very humbly and hopefully I went to Benares for a week at Christmas, in order to discover whether I might there find the bridge that I sought between East and West. I sat at Mrs. Besant's feet on various occasions, but on others I must admit I danced with two American tourists (one fair, one dark) whom I had met at the hotel. Looking back on them, even from this distance of time, I am not surprised that my attention should have been distracted from the holy city of the Hindus. It is true that I searched for Sivanand Joshi, and also attended the lectures at the Central Hindu College, but my pursuit of knowledge was not as diligent as it would have been had there not been a curly head, and a pair of bow-shaped lips, and a Virginian burr in my memory. But for this frailty I might have become wiser.

Or again, I might not.

As to Mrs. Besant, she was all that I had imagined her to be in eloquence, dignity, sincerity ; and Krishnamurti, whom the esoteric section of the Theosophists believed was about to become the Saviour of the World, seemed a modest, handsome, straightforward lad. But I was very much disappointed in their friends.

Before the meetings, a venerable figure (who was later accused of abducting the Theosophical Messiah, but acquitted) used to give us lithographed scraps of paper containing messages revealed to him by the Masters of the Great White Lodge. On their way from the snows of Tibet these thought-transferences seemed to me to have lost their sting and degenerated into platitudes. Krishnamurti generally sat on the platform with Mrs. Besant. On one occasion he spoke. As bad luck would have it I had made an appointment this evening to dine with my friends, so I missed a scene which may (or may not) be remembered as epochal in future ages. For it was then that the Holy Spirit descended on Krishnamurti. " Great vibrations thrilled through the hall," wrote an eye-witness afterwards in the *Theosophist*, " and the slender figure took on a surprising majesty. Indians, Europeans, Americans, bowed their heads at the feet of the sixteen-year-old Brahmin boy, whose body was shaken by the Coming Avatar, and asked his blessing." These things we missed for grilled chicken and Pol Roger.

I can never forget the debt I owe to Mrs. Besant. But the masters, the Great Ones, the Lords of Karma, and so on, were not for me. The fair and dark tourists taught me more of life.

CHAPTER VI

POLO

And now the scene changes to Naini Tal, a hill station near Bareilly, where I am playing in the final match of a polo tournament. The time is a summer afternoon of the late Edwardian age.

My ponies are Daim, Tot, Crediton, with Ur of the Chaldees as a reserve. I'll give Crediton his breather first. The white ball bounds before us : Crediton follows it without touch of rein or spur. Tap—tap—tap—I've dribbled it the length of the field and through the goal at full gallop. That is easier to do on this little Naini Tal polo ground than on a field of regulation size. Shall I be able to do it again in the match ?

Crediton has stopped, for he has seen the crowd and guesses that this is the final. He's sweating in front of his saddle and dancing from side to side; and now his muzzle's on the ground. He's bowing and scraping. . . . He's hysterical.

Now for Daim. You'll see the band from the middle of the ground, Daim, without standing on your hind legs. The noise puzzles you ? You shouldn't think so much ; it's bad for ponies. And why, oh why, do you have to twist your tongue over the bit ? Rubber can't hurt you.

Still five minutes to go. Joey is hitting the length of the small ground in a single stroke. I wish I could do that. Billy—our captain—is talking with the umpire. They're not nervous. They're both natural athletes, and both destined, as a matter of fact, to play for England against America—Joey three times.

Nothing has *happened* to my lunch. Soup, meat, trifle have undergone no diminution or digestion. Sick ? Yes, it's curious how Nature can make a violent effort of rejection when it would have been so much less trouble to deal with the meal in the usual way. And all this fuss is only about a game.

I'm sleepy now, with funk. Why don't we begin ? Flags and sun and people. I'm thick in the head.

I'll play Crediton first. None of your circus-tricks : this is serious. If I catch you bending . . . Rough-looking fellow, my opposing No. 1 with a red head to match his jersey and native-made breeches and boots too low. The umpire is holding up his hand. Beyond him I see parasols, white dresses, glitter. The ball's the thing.

"*Ride him, Y.B. !*"

Isn't that what I'm doing ? Crediton is leaning across the opposing No. 1. We bear down towards the umpire, tussling : he has only to put the ball at my feet and the game will begin. But he whistles, and turns, and sends us back. All to do again. I rein round in a daze. Shall I ever see the ball through this infernal sleep ? Now we are galloping in step towards the umpire—now—now—and now! The ball has flown past us in the air.

Joey has it. He turns, hits down the ground. "*Ride, Y.B.!*"

"Get out of my way, damn you!"

I am still entangled with No. 1. No hope of catching the back, who slashes down at the ball on his near side, returning it amongst us. Billy meets it and dribbles it again towards the enemy's goal.

"*Ride, Y.B.!*"

This time Crediton and I overtake the back so that he misses his return. With a clean crack Billy drives the ball forward, past us, towards goal. There is a thunder and a crying. The back and I are neck and neck. He is a big man, but his pony is out of hand, snatching at the bridle. Crediton leans on him, jerking his wise old head. My knee is behind my opponent's. His grip is loosening and I am forcing him off his saddle.

Billy is on the line of the ball, but he's being ridden-off. Joey, unmarked, bears down. The ball is six yards from goal, in its centre. Can he miss? Not Joey. He taps it through with a flick of the wrist: the whistle blows: we raise our sticks and yell for joy. First goal to us.

Cheers and fluttered handkerchiefs. Crediton faces the grand-stand and begins to kneel down again.

"Hurry up, Y.B.!"

"All right, all right!"

The umpire won't throw the ball straight. It has gone to their No. 2, who is off like a streak. The crowd cheers. The ball bounces off Joey's helmet, so that he can't hit a backhander. Bad luck that, for No. 2 is on it, and is tapping it round. He'll never do it at that pace. God, he has. He—has—— ! It's a goal !

Whistle. Yells. One all. We must begin again. No, Crediton ! That was a goal against us and *that's* what you get in the mouth for being an idiot.

Where's the ball ? Under my feet ?

" Get out ! "

" Go to hell ! "

" Get off it ! "

It's mine, out of the scrimmage. Hit or dribble ?

" *Ride, Y.B. !* "

Must I leave it ? God, that's hard !

Joey hits a glorious ball, clean and straight. Back and I are having a great fight. He curses me, for he is a portly man of nearly sixty, while I am bony and ruthless.

" Damn it, can't you hear the whistle ? "

Already ? I thought we had only just begun. Seven and a half minutes have passed. This is the end of the first chukkar.

What's the matter ? I swing my leg over Crediton's neck. It's his off fore. Lifting his gaiter, I feel his nobbly fetlock wet with blood. I run off the ground at his side, he on three legs.

"Well played, Y.B.," said Billy. I hardly touched the ball, but praise is sweet.

Daim is standing on his hind legs, again. I wish I didn't have temperamental ponies. Will Crediton be fit for another chukkar ? Khushal is wrapping his legs in hot bandages.

"Well played, Y.B.," says Joey.

They've both said it, to encourage me, of course. It does encourage me.

We line up where we stopped play. Daim is on his hind legs when the ball is thrown in, so that I can't reach it. Then he jumps six foot into space. But I have it, somehow. A tap now. We're off. We have the legs of the field. Just now I dribbled the ball the length of the ground : I must do it again. Hell's foundations quiver ! As my stick came down the ball bounced, or Daim did. Daim, you brute, we must bump the back.

Back won't be bumped. He's on a crafty Arab which turns on a sixpence and leaves Daim cavorting about alone. Wait till we race for the ball, and then you won't see us for dust.

Is this chukkar never going to end ? The last passed in a flash, now we seem to have been playing half an hour. My throat's dry, and the reins have rubbed my fingers raw.

"For God's sake mark your man, Y.B. ! "

I can't hold Daim, that's the truth. He needs two hands to stop him. There's the ball. I'll let the swine loose !

"Hi! Hi! God Almighty!"

Whistle. Foul against us.

"Man alive," says Billy, "you can't cross like that."

A dangerous foul. That means a goal to them. In silence we ride back behind our goal. All my fault.

Our opponents take up their positions fifty yards opposite us. The back has only to hit the ball through our undefended flags. Two whistles. That means the end of the second chukkar, so my misery will be continued in the next period.

"We're holding them," says Billy during the brief interval. "It can't be helped about the foul. Ride at him as soon as he begins to hit. You never know."

Tot feels like a battleship under me. I have had a sip of champagne. The band is playing Bonnie Dundee.

Back is making his stroke. He must be nervous with so much depending on him.

Ride! Can I hit a ball in mid-air? I've missed, but why is Joey yelling "*Played, Y.B.*"? He thinks I've hit it. Well, Tot has, with her hoof. Billy is on the ball now, and I'm marking my man as I should.

Up and down we race. I'm clinging desperately to the back, using him as a cushion. That's useful, anyway. Time. That period was quickly over. Is this match an agony, or is it bliss undreamed of? One all, and half time.

Can I ride Crediton again? He's better on three legs than Daim on four. But Billy says that I must keep

Crediton for the last chukkar. So my choice is between Ur of the Chaldees or that indiarubber son of a gun, Daim, who's cut my hands to ribbons. Khushal has tied his tongue down now. It lolls out bluely, still over the bit. I'll give him a trial. Yes, Brownstone ; it's one all. Can't you read the numbers ? Water on the back of my neck : how good it feels, dripping.

I think we'll win, if I don't disgrace myself.

The opposing one trots out lame, goes back. We wait. He has reappeared on a black carthorse. That's his reserve pony probably.

I've got the ball this time at last, and have tapped it forward to Billy under Daim's neck. Up and down, up and down. Will the ball never come to me ? I'm enjoying myself, though, bumping the back over the side-lines, and turning under the carthorse's nose. Here's a backhander for me to hit—and I've hit it too, for once in a blue moon. Daim, you jewel ! Joey has the ball. Will he—won't he ? No, his shot goes wide. My stick's broken. A spare stick—quick ! They have hit out from behind, and No. 2 swoops down to our goal amidst a ripple of clapping.

Goal to them, almost before I knew what was happening. Time. That's the end of the fourth chukkar and the score's two–one against us.

" I wish to God you'd keep on the ground and try to hit the ball," says Joey.

Yes, I know his censure is deserved.

Billy slices to the side wall as soon as we begin again: Joey takes the rebound with a near-side shot. Two inches more to the right, and it would have been a goal.

"Meet it, can't you?"

I can't. Tot is slow on her helm. My stick weighs a ton. These seven minutes are seven hours.

The last period. It is only forty minutes since I began this living. . . . Crediton, poor, sweet, good angel! If you die it will be in a good cause, but you won't, for this game's gone to your head, making you more than a horse. Steady. We've met it, by God!

I wish everyone would stop shouting. I know I've got to hit that spot of white. The goal flags are a little to my left. Now is our chance, Crediton! You are smooth and steady and fast; no one can catch us.

I am alone in the world with an open goal in front. A steady shot: a calm shot amidst the hoof-beats and cheers. I can't bring my stick down. It's stuck. Oh cruel, my stick has been hooked from behind. I'm helpless. The inviting ball bobs by; but Billy, bless him, is behind. And following him, trying to hook his stick, comes the red-headed No. 1. His hat's fallen off. Will the umpire stop the game? I can't look or listen. Back and I surge through the goal-flags, scattering a group of spectators who shout even as they run, for Billy has sent the ball true and straight, whizzing past my face.

We're level. Two all and six minutes to play. There's

Jagwant, solemn and tall. He is among a group who are waving their turbans—regimental servants. The crowd is a wild beast roaring for its food.

Quick back to the line-up. Crediton is lame at the trot, but can forget his pain. I must get the ball again. Yes, no, yes—I pass it to Billy, who shoots, but the wind carries it wide.

The game is becoming sticky with tension.

" Don't stand on the ball ! "

" Get to hell out of it ! "

Crediton could creep under these scrums. Yes, we've nosed-in among the sticks, and are out with the ball.

But a bugle sounds, and I hesitate. The umpire is shouting to me to play on (for the rule is that when we are level we continue until the ball goes out) but I have missed my stroke and the ball trickles over the back line. That ends the period.

After a minute's interval, we shall continue until one of us scores. I'll ride Daim again, my fastest pony, chastened now by hard work.

" Stick to the back, Y.B. ! " says Billy, " I'll meet the ball." So be it.

When the umpire throws in, I hurl myself at my opponent. Billy has it. No, it is Joey, and he is taking it to the centre of the ground. Why, he's standing still ! For an instant, that seems spun out to years, Joey stands there, a tower of blue and ivory, supremely sure of himself, glancing now at goal and now at two opponents who are turning on him. He taps the ball tenderly in front of his pony's forelegs, he aims, he brings his stick down with a crack that echoes yet in memory.

The driven ball sails low and swift. I've reined up to stare at Victory as she steals inch by inch over my senses.

Daim shies away towards the back whom he has been so cheerfully bumping, for he understands riding-off, but not this voice of a ranging beast that is coming from all round us. How did Joey carve that second out of eternity? How has he conquered time? The ball is still in the air : as it reaches the goal-posts it rises and soars between them. The goal umpire is gripping his signal flag. He's waved it. Finish !

People are running all over the ground. We've won ! That's all, Daim. Bran mash for you. *Baksheesh* for the servants. The syces will get drunk, I suppose.

Head in a bucket. Shake hands with Khushal. Jagwant is salaaming, rather lower than usual, but still impassive. Joey has lamed two ponies, and Billy one. Now we must go to receive the cup from the Lieutenant-Governor. You've got the *baksheesh* money, Khushal ? Good. I'll borrow that comb.

A red-faced man has heaved himself out of a wicker chair and is handing a silver bowl to Billy.

Hand-shaking with our opponents. We are dining with them at the Club, before the dance to-night.

We fight our battles over again at the bar. Back shows me his bruises : he is a tea-planter with a great thirst. Three whiskey-and-sodas is a good foundation for dinner—or isn't it ? Another ? I don't mind. I do mind, but it can't be helped. My stomach shall be back's sacrifice.

But nothing will induce me to go on to the Lieutenant-Governor's ball. I have had enough of crowds.

When the dandy coolies arrive to carry us to Government House, someone says : " We'll race to the L.-G.'s."

That's a good idea. I'll be the starter.

They're off, swinging down the path to the Boat Club. The mellow voices, of men who have dined well fade away and the jigging lights of seven hurricane lamps grow small. The procession is crossing the polo ground now—a shout comes up through the firs as one lamp passes another.

Here's five rupees for my dandy coolies : they can go to bed or pick up a chance fare.

I'm alone in the grateful dark.

The Club smoking-room, through which I must pass to reach my bedroom, is deserted save for an ancient Colonel, who is smoking a cheroot with a straw down the middle, and drinking white curaçao.

"Not dancin'?"

"Not yet. I'm going to look round my ponies first."

The dogs are waiting for me: the puppies waddling crabwise towards Daisy's teats, Daisy looking like Diana of the Ephesians, Brownstone in a prancing mood, his great paws striking this way and that. He is a perfect friend, too good for me, all twisted up as I am in fancies and philosophies. He never thinks, but lives and loves and feeds and fights. . . .

Brownstone and I go down to see the ponies, who have supped on bran and linseed and molasses.

Crediton staled blood after he hobbled home, Khushal says, but he has no fever, and he has just drunk two buckets of barley water. Daim's tongue is badly cut, but his appetite is unimpaired. Tot is lying at full stretch, relaxed, a picture of equine content. I put a carrot under her nose. She snuffles it, gobbles, sighs dreamily. Ur is wide awake; he cocks one ear back and the other forward, and turns his upper lip backward in a grin, clowning for attention. I enter his stall to pat him. He rushes to the corner in simulated terror, ears flat back, off heel raised. I slap him hard: he turns and nips the air, then muzzles into the haversack in which Khushal carries carrots and sugar.

Below us, the syces are banqueting by firelight. They have six hill-women with them and they all seem sober.

I wish I was. This life I lead is a drunkenness in itself, an intoxication whose natural complement is strong food and drink. To-night I've had too much of it ; too much of everything.

Good-night, Khushal, I'm tired. Does he notice I'm not walking straight ? He can't help smelling drink, with his unpolluted senses. But most of us smell of alcohol and tobacco.

Up and up, with Brownstone panting at my heels. Drink and dinner is being blown out of me. Brownstone has his second wind : ten days ago he thought he couldn't walk in the hills, but now he has caught my mood. We are following the path that leads to the crest of Cheena, behind the Club. Soon we shall be above the houses of Naini Tal.

" The albatross knows its way about the sea better than the most experienced captain." Where did I read that ? It is true. Instinct is better than knowledge. My life as a soldier is jolly enough while it lasts, but its pleasures are as fickle as the fumes of champagne. Here on the mountains, alone with my thoughts and my dog, I am sober again.

The Himalayas stand up before me in the moonlight, so close, so high, that I catch my breath as I lift my eyes to them.

Dear mountains which India has worshipped since the dawn of history, before your mighty towers and turrets, your lonely heights and snows, your music of tree and water, I am humbled and content. I bless your silence and peace, cities of the Aryan soul.

Far below that white and blinding beauty, gleams the lake of Naini Tal. By its shores, and along the huddled houses, lights wink and pass. On the opposite mountain glows a replica of the night sky of London, from the invisible Government House, where there are medals, bows, whispers, pride, painted faces.

And here, in a grotto by the pathway, is a shrine. I strike a match. Brownstone stands on his hind legs, and together we peer at the red symbol of Siva, decked with a garland of marigolds. Above it, roughly carved out of the rock, his slender-waisted and great-breasted goddess, smiles with her full lips and her long eyes, as she writhes in her ceremonial dance. She is his *shakti*, or creative aspect.

To live we must be created. That is how we may become aware of eternity. Siva is the Lord of Change : his consort is the Mistress of Time : their children do not grow up, or age, or die : but change. That is all, and everything. Brownstone puffs and wheezes beside me, a link with sanity, contemptuous of the gods of desire who drive the world.

These little games I play, and all this striving and scheming and sorrow, make up the world in which Brownstone and I pass as phantoms. Soon the lights of Government House will be swallowed up, and its bricks will crumble, and all our works of power and pride will be transmuted to colloidal particles and gases. In the twinkling of Siva's eye.

These mountains on which Brownstone and I are standing, the greatest in the world, will be worn away rock by rock, in the revolution of the centuries, as Siva and his consort tread their measure, until at last this Age is danced away, and Brahm, wearying of His world, shall sleep.

Change and fixed purpose ; names and forms dissolving and reappearing ; an infinite beauty and a precision beyond imagining through all kinds of apparent cruelty and confusion ; a stirring in the womb of night ; a glimmer out of nescience ; sleep again—that is this world of desire and death. Sleep. We may know that as reality, my dog and I.

Soon the sun will flood the Ganges in a glow of gold and turn to vermeil the white domes of Delhi. Before me Ushas, the twilight maid, type of all the loves of Earth unsatisfied, will drive her chariot through the east ; and Surya, her lover, will rise from his haunts in the nether world to pursue the light of morning knowledge. We shall wake to more pain, more pleasure.

But to-night as I lie stretched on these pine needles, the desire of experiencing has left me utterly. Mother Earth has emptied my head of thoughts and Brownstone's jowl is on my chest.

CHAPTER VII

PIGSTICKING

Half a dozen of us are lying inert on camp-beds behind mosquito curtains, in the big banyan grove, near Ratmugri Bagh. We are listening to the prelude to another day's pigsticking—beaters chattering to each other as gun-wads are distributed to them as tokens exchangeable for their daily wage of twopence, servants quarrelling for amusement, the cook pelting a prowling village dog, the dignified burbling of the camel which is being saddled for its journey to the railway station to bring ice and letters.

There is the Shikari, tall, grey bearded, with Græcian profile coming to tell the Tent Club Secretary of the prospects of sport. You can see by his bearing that he carries in him the *genes* of a conquering race (the Robilla Pathans) but he is as much a native of these plains as any of the Hindu beaters whom he curses so heartily and picturesquely in the idiom of the country. With him are two elders of the Tent Club staff known as Paderewski and Kubelik.

They are remarkable old men, these wild-haired headmen of the Nuts. Respectable villages will have nothing to do with the Nuts, for they are a Criminal

Tribe, whose men are professional thieves, and whose women are whores, yet for all that they are a decent people. They might engage in much more profitable business than the beating-out of pig for us to ride, but sport is more to them than money, and they are content to toll all day for a pittance with the Tent Club, often in peril of their lives. Civic virtues they lack, but fortunately there is more than one standard of worth in this world.

Our horses are saddled, and the two elephants are ready—Moti Lal with his howdah and crate of lager beer packed in wet straw, and Lashkman Piari with her pad, on which nothing but a medicine chest is carried. If there should be a casualty, it will be her office to convey the sufferer to hospital.

Last night I gave her a rupee for herself. She went to the neighbouring village, dropped the money into the *baniah's* lap and helped herself to as much sugar-cane as she could carry in her trunk. Now she opens her mouth and raises her trunk sky-high in an impressive *salaam*. She is a snob, like most elephants, and thinks I'm rich.

Moti Lal is not so sure of me. Moti Lal belongs to a Rajah (whereas Piari's master is only a *zamindar*) and attends all the *tamashas* of the district—marriages, festivals, tiger-shoots. He had seen two generations of men come and go, and has salaamed to two Viceroys and knelt to a King. He is old and conservative, and dislikes the look of Brownstone. None of the great men he has met had a dog like this.

There is a cool wind from the hills, and a scent of flowering bamboos from a near-by *bagh.* What if the butter is rancid and the eggs stink? Sun and air are food on these marvellous plains.

The Shikari has mounted his flea-bitten mare. The Nuts, with their mongrel dogs, move off in a separate group to the other beaters, for they consider themselves a caste superior to the villagers while pigsticking is in progress.

After drawing lots for our positions, we separate into " heats " and ride off to our appointed places. We are to beat Ratmugri Bagh first, a glade of linked bamboo thickets, full of shade and water and good rootling-grounds. In its pools several *bahut bhari baba* have been seen wallowing at their ease—" very heavy grandfather pig "—and we are reasonably certain of good sport.

My first horse to-day is The Devil, a bright bay country-bred, out of an Arab mare by a thorough-bred English stallion. He is the best charger I have ever owned.

While the beaters are tapping their slow way through the thicket, he lifts his beautiful head; nostrils wide, ears cocked; hearing, smelling, seeing, every nerve tense as he dances round and round my bridle hand. Two peacocks prance out of a ride, screech, flap back to the village. Dust-whirls dance in the yellow plain, shimmering away to the pale goddesses of the Himalayas. Leaves and branches stir to a light wind. It is good to be alive on such a day, with pipe in mouth and a good horse ready. A sow looks out of her shelter, goes back, gathers her family together—six blue-black babies with a gold band round their bellies—and leads them all out past us not twenty yards away. They stop when The Devil snorts. He wonders why I don't mount and ride?

The squeakers stand stuffily, wondering who we are and what we want. When they are older, they'll know. The Devil quits prancing and pawing, for he has guessed, I think, that they are too small. He sniffs the air, snatches nervously at some grass, jerks up his head again to listen to the yelping of the Nuts' dogs. I can recognise the voices of Jim (the terrier) and Majira (the semi-dachshund bitch) and Bachu (the half-Airedale). Yes, Bachu has stirred a boar out of his sleep. Bang! That's the Shikari's blunderbuss, to speed the parting guest. One, two three, come the sounders out of the *bagh*, with a dozen pig in each.

God, how glorious! The plain is black with pig, and amongst them are at least half a dozen rideable boar. My heat has swung into saddle without a word. We don't ride yet, however, for we must give the quarry time to break clear of cover.

The Devil's heart is drumming between my legs.

Lashkman Piari comes crashing out of the *bagh* at a

trot. Her mahout takes off his yellow turban and waves it and yells to us as if we hadn't seen the six big boar and their thirty brothers and sisters streaming across the *maidan* under our noses.

Now another two sounders have broken towards the group at the far side of the *bagh*, a mile away, and are making along the canal. I can see the riders mount and cram down their hats and raise their spears. Through the heat-waves the sun looks distant and fantastic—*maya*, maybe?—that Becoming which is not illusion. The notion flickers in my mind and is extinguished, for the time has come to ride.

We're off, each after a boar of his own. Mine is a big red one. I cram heels to The Devil and we eat up the ground between us and our prey.

But as soon as he sees that he is being pursued, down goes his head and up his heels, with a spurt of dust behind them. He is making for Khaitola, a *bagh* some two miles away. If he keeps to that line I shall certainly kill him, for it is open going and The Devil can overtake even a lean young boar within a mile. This one is fat, and obviously short in wind and temper.

He begins to tire, and sits down so suddenly that I can't stop. As I pass, reining hard, I see his little blood-shot eyes with the hate of the world in them, and his lips' wicked lines, snarling back from a pair of remarkably fine tushes. He is up again by the time I have turned The Devil, and is making for some road menders' pits near the river. It is foul going here ; he stumbles and rips at the earth that tripped him.

Then he sees a tethered goat, and disembowels it in his rage. Just with a flick of his neck as he gallops by !

The goat is done for. I must stop. Poor goat—what a fate—what a mess ! A thrust to the heart, and it is out of its pain.

That has lost me several lengths, but now the boar is loitering again. He is one of the red, truculent sort for which Bareilly is famous, who would sooner fight than run. As we draw up, he stops, about turns, charges. It all happens so invisibly-quick that I can hardly put my spear down. We meet at eighty miles an hour and my spear-point strikes the top of his skull, grazing down his shoulder. There is a jar, a scuffle. I turn The Devil with an oath and an unkind hand on the bit.

The boar has trotted to a bush where only the ridge of his back is visible. I have at him again, but The Devil's thoroughbred skin is so delicate that he refuses to face the thorns. Five, ten minutes I wait, cursing myself for a clumsy fool.

The Shikari canters up on his old grey mare. Behind him comes Lashkman Piari and some of the Nuts. The Shikari is very angry. Why did I stop to kill the goat ? This is the best boar in Ratmugri Bagh. Unless I have wounded him badly he will recover his wind and make a dash for the river and get away. Shall I go in on foot,

I ask him? "Don't be a fool, Sahib," growls the old man, waving to the elephant.

Lashkman Piari ambles up with a distinct smile behind her trunk. Why she enjoys this business no man knows. She is as nervous as a kitten on a bridge, dithers at slippery going, and becomes idiotic with fright at a quicksand, yet when bidden to stamp on a wounded boar—the most dangerous brute in creation—she is transformed into an Amazon and a heroine.

The Devil is snatching at his bridle, and nibbling grass again, trembling, in a lather of foam. Piari, with her trunk lifted out of harm's way, heaves her big feet about among the thorns. *Woof!* The boar is away, making for the river, as the Shikari said. I am on his tail, though. He can't escape me now, for I am between him and his goal.

Almost I'm sorry, because the advantages are all on my side. Yet the boar is too noble for pity. I see him calculating the moment that he will charge: "Give me liberty or give me death!" My spear is well down this time. He throws himself on it. A fountain of blood jets up. He is dead, only about a hundred yards from his sanctuary.

In the open, the odds are against the boar, but in blind cover he has more than an equal chance against a man. That is one of the purifying risks of pigsticking.

The other two of my heat have wounded a thirty-six inch boar who lies in a patch of thick thorn. We must go in on foot. The elephants cannot push their way into the tangle and it would not be fair to ask the beaters to risk themselves. Three of us, therefore, creep to his lair.

The dogs have been leashed. It is dark where we are. In front of me something grunts, crashes, splinters wood. The man on my right gasps ; he has been charged and knocked down. A small wound in his breeches drips blood ; his spear is broken.

We work round again to the boar. There he is grunting and crashing and charging—but whom ? A disorderly pulse hammers in my throat.

I smell pig overpoweringly. A great head, each bristle on it distinct, confronts me out of the thorns. Something hits me in the ribs ; it is the butt of my spear, which the boar has driven into me as he passed. I've wounded him, but far back. I run to the edge of the bushes and see him struggling out, treading on his bowels.

He makes for Paderewski, who attempts to avoid the charge by jumping up his pole. The boar trips (for he is spent and dying) and falls on his knees. Before he rolls over jerks at Paderewski.

Lashkman Piari hurries up with the medicine chest. Paderewski is holding his leg tightly, for his thigh is cut to the bone. The Tent Club Secretary gives him half a tumbler of brandy, then a little ether. I dissolve a pellet of disinfectant in soda water. He is white to the lips under his brown skin, but this kind of thing is all in the day's work ; he has suffered a score of woundings in our service.

The veins knot at his temples, but he does not wince when I feel his leg for a fracture. Nothing is broken this time, and the stitches can wait for the hospital. What's that stuff to stop bleeding ? Hyoscine. A wad of that, and now we hoist him on to the pad elephant. He brushes back the long hair tumbling over his eyes with one hand, and stretches out the other for more brandy, grinning, undismayed at his twenty-first mishap. He will get no less than sixpence a day of blood money while he is being mended.

The Sahib comes next. His wound is larger than we thought, but only half an inch deep, looking like a streak of lightning on the inner side of his thigh. We put him beside Paderewski on the elephant and send them both back to camp.

Now Moti Lal yields up his stores of lager beer and damp cheroots. The beaters squat round in a circle, nibbling grain and parched barley. Three boar have been killed this morning, and they are well content, although none of them has more in his belly than there is in a London pigeon's. Twopence a day is not much, even in India, but they have seen good sport from the shade of Ratmugri. Now a harder-earned pennyworth of work is in store for them, for we are to draw the grass country by the Ganges, and they will have to walk miles and miles, knowing that every step they take they may tread on a pig, panther, or even the King of the Jungle himself. No doubt they will have much to tell their wives this evening.

The Devil goes back to camp, where barley water and hot bandages await him. He whinnies and looks back as he is led away, as if to say that one run is nothing for a big horse with a light-weight in the saddle. That's true, but he is too precious to risk so early in the season.

Ur of the Chaldees is also a country-bred, slower of foot, but quicker of brain. Indeed he is as clever as a man, and thinks more than is good for a horse—qualities inherited from the Arab sire. In blind country I can always trust him to pick his way ; and on the tail of a pig he knows exactly where to place himself. When we fall, which is often, he stands patiently beside me, waiting to be mounted again. A bit is unnecessary in his mouth ; nothing but a white rope-halter has adorned his intelligent face for more than a year now. If he were only a little faster, he might win me the Kadir Cup.

On a small scale, this *jhow* pigsticking is like the hunting circle of the Mongols,[1] who drove every living thing before them, gradually drawing in their line for a great slaughter, followed by a great feast. Our quarry is the boar, but everything else in the jungle flies in front of our horses ; hog-deer who scuttle between

[1] The *Kurultai*.

beaters' legs, and hares, and cyrus-cranes, whose staid flirtations it seems boorish to interrupt, and wild cattle, *nilgai*, peacocks, panther. . . .

A group of beaters, sauntering by a grass-fringed stream, have stopped and run together like frightened sheep. The Shikari gallops up ; but his mare plants her forelegs and refuses to move, for she smells what is lurking there.

With a snarling that freezes my blood, a panther flashes by me in a streak of gold. We pursue him, but the *jhow* is so tall that it hides even our horses, and he is soon lost to view, which is just as well, perhaps, for there are only two men alive who can face a panther with their hog-spear, and be sure of killing him. Now the beaters go forward again lightheartedly. A kingfisher dives smartly into the Ganges. The shadow of a hawk passes over the wet sand.

I am feeling thirsty, and ride down a rutty road to a village, past a mango-grove where monkeys gibber. A yellow and white dog squirms and barks when I reach the little mud houses of Shikarpur ; a water buffalo lowers its long horns ; women at the well veil themselves. I am an unwelcome intruder. One of the girls is young and beautiful ; I ask her for water, but she shivers, and presses both hands to her face and turns to the wall. Is that coquetry, or convention ? I am as innocent as I am thirsty.

I explain my need to a merchant, who comes out of

his shop salaaming, white as the flour he sells. He searches for an earthenware vessel, and gives me to drink. But I do not tarry, for I know that I am not wanted here.

I am hated in this kind village. The doves flutter scatheless round the village shrine ; peacock tread the earth delicately and proudly, knowing that they are held precious ; even the monkeys that loot the *baniahs'* shops are sacred ; but this white monkey that has ridden into the village on a stamping horse, grasping a hog-spear, has brought pollution with the very air he breathes. The cup from which he has drunk will be broken.

I am back with the line in time to see a pig break to another heat. Six hours we have been in saddle—and the last three without a hunt. Yet I could go on like this for ever with the magic of the Ganges plains before me. Here land and air are wide and worthy of giants. The crops, the soft-eyed oxen, the far horizon, the white masses of its north-eastern limit, the dim blue *baghs* to southward, the pig, and peacock, and panther, and scurrying deer ; all sights and sounds under this turquoise vault, except mankind, are heart of my heart and carry in some mysterious fashion memories of another life. A life in which the freedom of the villages was also mine.

Riding with me is the Civil Magistrate of the district, a good sportsman and a good officer, loved by his people.

" Do you think," I ask him, " that it is possible to know India—I mean the life of the peasants ? "

" It is possible, but unwise," he says. " The people don't ask for friendship, but fairness. They want some-one from the outside to judge them. All that is necessary is to be accessible to them when they come with their complaints."

"And that isn't as easy as it seems, I suppose? Do you think for instance, that these villagers of yours have to bribe their way to your presence ? "

" I hope not," he says : " for I ride about the district a great deal. Of course I know there is a danger that my servants may take *baksheesh*. But I have an old retainer whom I trust. He comes with me everywhere."

" That old man ? " I ask, nodding to a grey-beard who follows us with a *chowri*, to keep off the flies.

" Yes, I trust him absolutely."

The Collector has hardly spoken, before a peasant flings himself under our horses' feet.

" I have only four rupees," sobs the suppliant, " for years I have been trying to bring my case to you."

" Four rupees ? "

" Yes, Cherisher of the Poor, that man "—pointing to the patriarch with the fly-whisk—" wants five rupees to allow me to enter your Court."

That evening, after we have finished drawing the *jhow*, an enormous swarm of pig—a line at least half a mile in length—comes streaming out of Khaitola Bagh. It charges through a herd of cattle, scattering them in all directions, and darkens the plain with bodies of all sizes and both sexes. Each of us has marked down a monster for his prey. Mine is a beauty. Ur cocks his ears, I do believe he's judging its weight.

He's a fast boar too. Ur can't gain on him at first. Khaitola Bagh is close. If he jinks now, I'm done. I wish I had The Devil !

At last we draw level. Then, a foot too far away to spear him safely, my quarry turns in a right-angled left-handed jink. I flatten myself in the saddle, and thrust at him, across Ur's forelegs. Crash ! Flump ! Where am I ?

My mouth is full of dust and my nose of pig. I'm pinned to the ground, face down, and there's a most unpleasant pain in my legs. I can't move them. Twisting my neck, I see the sweat-lathered hide of Ur, looming above me. His rope halter is in my left hand, torn off his head. Well, if that is all that is broken . . . Ur is struggling to get up, damn him. The pig is on his other side, transfixed by my spear, which is also under Ur's body. A carrion hawk observes us three unwilling bed-fellows, expecting something.

I can only wait.

My thoughts go back to England, where I hope to be,

come May year. I have lost a tooth. I wish I had a quart of lager beer. Ur shall have a bottle too, if we get out of this mess. Lawn tennis is a good game—it doesn't jar. The Adjutancy—promising young officer cut short in his career—paralysis ? My brain is buzzing like a clockwork mouse. I wish Ur would either get up or lie down. I'd rather die quick than continue in this pain.

The pig is wriggling himself off the spear. I must think straight. Run straight, I mean, if I get the chance. Now Ur's heaved himself up. He's nibbling grass, the idiot.

Can I run ?

Can't I ? There's a tree.

I don't know how I've come here.

Does this swollen blue thumb belong to me ?

The pig is dead with my broken spear in him, and the earth is heaving under him. And under Ur too, who is grazing in a billowy plain, with his saddle twisted under his belly. Men and horses and elephants are approaching through an earthquake.

With a wet towel round my head, I am allowed to attend the evening ceremony of weighing and measuring our five mighty boar. Those of us who have obtained a "first spear" examine the tushes of their victims, while our syces press round us, watchfully, for it is their perquisite to take away the bristles along the spine, and various other parts, one of which is reputed to be an aphrodisiac. When all the particulars have been entered into the Tent Club log, the bodies are given to the Nuts, who will cut them up and gorge themselves on pork to-night.

Then there is the paying of coolies. A hundred men squat before us in a semi-circle ; each holding a gun-wad in his right hand. The Tent Club Secretary has a stick and a bag of money, the Shikari, a lantern, for it is growing dark. The Secretary counts the men, while the Shikari collects the gun-wads ; every eighth man is tapped with a stick, which is a signal for him to rise and receive a rupee to divide with the seven beaters on his left.

Finally we attend to casualties, not only our own but any sick folk of the neighbourhood who care to come. Our methods are quick, drastic, popular. No medicine which does not taste horrible is administered. Quinine we mix with asafœtida ; itch we cure with neat sulphuric acid ; purgatives we have a-plenty, and ginger ; and Easton's syrup, but only for eminent and elderly preservers of pig. For miles round our fame has spread. One of our members is a distinguished surgeon ; we allow him to deal with the difficult cases, but the Secretary and I are more popular as consulting physicians.

Paderewski needs a great deal of brandy, poor old chap, and is given enough to put a guardsman to sleep. Then Lashkman Piari's mahout comes to report she is feverish, and as it has been a good day he is given half a bottle of whiskey, which he solemnly shares with her. Ur sups off a Bass and cooked barley.

For me there is no dinner to-night. I lie on my bed near the mess-table contentedly enough, listening to the tales of the veterans ; how the great hog of Saidupur jumped upon the back of a horse ; how the gods of the temple by the curving stream of Shahi were propitiated by *baksheesh* before we drew the covert ; how Wardrop manages the Meerut Tent Club ; how Faunthorpe kills panthers ; how we speared ten boar on the sunlit plain of Kicha ; and of the prowess of those great horses Sausage and Cowdapple, and Bohemian, and Fizzer—a saga of stories that will never be written.

By my bed lies the Abbé Dubois' *Hindu Manners and Customs* to remind me that I once met a pundit who told me of a nephew of his. The book, however, remains outside the mosquito curtain. Instead of reading, I sharpen my hogspear.

I file away with my swollen hand, and spit blood. When I lie flat, the bed rocks gently, as if I were floating.

CHAPTER VIII

MEN AND MUD TURTLES

One morning, after I had become Adjutant of my regiment, I noticed on recruits' parade an Afridi shepherd lad, round-thighed and awkward in the saddle, who was rolling off his horse like the White Knight.

His ride was in the jumping lane : at each obstacle Naim Shah (for his mother had named him " Merciful King ") leant forward, snatched the reins in his mutton fist, and jerked them so that he cut his horse's mouth. I put him on another horse and the same thing happened.

His new horse was an easy one. I rode it over the jumps myself to show him how simple was the task I asked him to perform (forgetting that I had ten years' experience and he ten weeks) and I explained that he and I would stay here all day, if need be, until he stopped funking.

He scowled at that, but it was necessary to be firm, for if a beginner loses his nerve, he may never regain it. I sent the rest of the ride away, and ordered him to mount. He hesitated. I jumped off my horse and stood by him with my hunting-crop, and called him a coward, and worse. We were man to man in a sense, for I would have fought him level and probably been worsted physically had he mutinied. But unfair advantages were on my side—my rank and experience against his innocence and ignorance—the military system against a sense of what is decent between man and man in a free country.

He mounted in a dumb rage. Not content with his sulky obedience, I lashed his horse's quarters, sending it careering over the first two jumps. His long body leant first this way, then that. At the third jump, after the turn in the lane, he would infallibly have been unseated, but the horse (infected as animals sometimes are by a contagion of human emotion) instead of keeping to the track galloped straight ahead, and tried to jump the enclosing wall. Failing to clear it, it hung for a moment, balanced on its belly, half in and half out of the lane. Naim Shah still sat with his arms crossed. Then the wall collapsed, and he was crushed against it.

My heart stood still. Rage melted into pity, and hate into love. He lay on the tan, with the horse beside him, entangled in reins and stirrup leathers. The Drill Major and I pulled him out, dazed. I knew it would be worse than useless to say anything at the moment. So I sent him back to his ride of recruits.

Later in the morning, I told him in the presence of his comrades that he was excused foot drill for a week. But he only looked at me in a curious sullen way, meditating revenge.

That night, as I lay on my bed in the open air, hot

and restless, and not at all well pleased with myself, some impulse made me get up and go back into the verandah.

What I expected to find there I do not know, but what I did find was Naim Shah, in the shadow, hesitating, bare-headed, with turban round his loins, as is the habit of Afridis when raiding. I went to him, and took both his arms at the wrist. " *Se de, wror me ?*—What is it, brother ? " I asked.

He began to stammer. To-morrow was Saturday. His troop commander (a cousin of his) wanted to borrow my rifle for black-buck shooting. He had not wanted to disturb me.

" Did he send you to me—at night ? "

" Yes."

It was a lie, but rather a good one, for the troop commander did sometimes borrow my rifle. Naim Shah had come for another purpose. We stood still, close to each other, so that I felt what he did not say.

" Come inside, brother, and tell me what is the matter."

We went to a long chair, and he sat down on its arm beside me.

" Thou hast made my face black," he said, using the pronoun of equals.

" I am sorry for it, as you must know."

Silence.

" You have a knife under your coat," I said.

" Yes, Sahib."

" Discipline is a hard thing. But it is necessary in the Army, because officers are not perfect. You must do as you are told, even when you are wrongly abused."

" In my country a man would be killed for speech like thine."

" You are young, and so am I. Let us be friends."

The tap of the night-watchman's stick came to my ears. Naim Shah sat there wordless, his eyes wet.

" How did you get in without being seen ? " I asked.

" I am an Afridi," he sobbed. Then, as if that had explained everything, he added " The *chowkidar* mustn't know that I am here. It might be misunderstood."

I was silent until the night-watchman had clip-clopped away.

" I know why you came, Naim Shah, and what you wanted to do," I said. " Let's forget it."

" You were right to call me a coward, Sahib. Otherwise——"

He unbuttoned his coat and showed me the dagger he carried, smiling as he tested the needle-like point on his finger.

" It was common sense, not cowardice, that kept that in its place," I said. " Why make such a fuss ? "

" Sahib, shall I ever be able to ride ? "

" Not only will you be a roughrider, Naim Shah, but

within a year I will make you my orderly, if you behave yourself. Now go the way you came. And——"

" Yes, Sahib ?

Breast to breast and knee to knee we took leave of each other.

For months I did not speak to him again.

Before the year was out, however, he had proved to be the best recruit of his class. The Colonel marked him for promotion (without any recommendation from me) and he would have become a lance corporal but for the fact that he steadfastly refused to learn to read and write. Scholarship bred worms in the brain, he told the Drill Major. So when Khushal Khan left the regiment on the death of his father to look after his property, Naim Shah reigned in his stead, and brought with him his young brother, Sher Dil, a lively lad of eleven.

This little Lion-Heart (for that was the meaning of his name) had love-locks curling down from either ear, and the features of a Donatello angel. He and Naim Shah were like a double almond, always together. Wherever I went with the regimental polo team, Sher Dil would come too, as a mascot and stick-holder.

One evening in Calcutta, where we had gone to play in the Championship Tournament, it occurred to me that Sher Dil was likely to fall into evil ways, exposed as he was to the temptations of a great city and a vagabond life.

"Sher Dil," I said, "why aren't you at school instead of sucking the thumb of idleness?"

Sher Dil didn't know.

"Why isn't he at school?" I asked Naim Shah. "This life is bad for him. Who paid his fare in the train?"

"No one paid his fare, Sahib. He travels with the horses, and refuses to go to school."

"Refuses! He is no bigger than a mongoose, and refuses to go to school! . . . Without book-knowledge, Sher Dil, you will remain poor, like your foolish brother. But if you learn to read and write you may easily earn fifty rupees a month by driving a motor car."

"I don't want to drive a motor car, Sahib, but to be always with you."

"*Shaitan-ka-bacha*, by the time you are a man I shall have left this country. Put no faith in me, or any Sahib. Stand on your own feet. There is no power and no virtue save in the Most High.

"You spoil your brother," I said to Naim Shah. "Why *don't* you send him to school? Is there any reason except your prejudice? Look at Rissaldar Hamzullah Khan. Learning hasn't done him any harm."

" Sahib, you don't know Sher Dil," Naim Shah answered thoughtfully.

I admitted that.

" Then you must know," said Naim Shah, " that before I brought him down into India, he quarrelled with Gul Must, my youngest brother, may God give him peace. Sher Dil had a hunting knife, and to give point to his argument, he stuck it into his brother's belly. Gul Must died. Sher Dil was surprised, but he said nothing about it to any of us, and he hid him in a thorn bush. In the fort that night, Gul Must was missing. We asked Sher Dil where his brother was. He said he had not seen him. But some other boys told us that they had been playing together. So we went out and found the body. Then Sher Dil confessed, and he confessed also that he had tried to set fire to the bush. When the Malik heard that, he called a council to consider whether he should be put to death, for to burn the body of a son of Adam is a very shameful thing. But I pleaded with the elders and showed them that Sher Dil was a pious child, for even then he could repeat both the Fatiha and the Cow[1] by heart. Now he knows all the Koran Sherif. So the *jirga* decided to exile Sher Dil to British India. That is why I brought him down to you. No one except my relations knows about his blood-guilt, Sahib, even in the squadron."

" Certainly Sher Dil must go to school," I said when

[1] The first two chapters of the Holy Koran.

I heard this story, " and if he becomes as learned as he is pious, I daresay he'll be a great man."

I wonder what did happen to Sher Dil? I lost sight of him in the war, but heard later that he had enlisted in 1918 in the Supply and Transport Corps as a " boy follower." Neither Naim Shah nor I have been able to trace him : he has disappeared : he may be dead now, or he may be a rich contractor. Much will have been forgiven him for the sake of his *beaux yeux*.

I was very busy with the Adjutancy this year of 1912, and anchored to a mass of pale brown paper.

Who that has served in India does not know those mind-defeating documents beginning: " Will you kindly refer to this office memo. O.P./110/26713 dated 15.2.30 " and ending " for favour of necessary action " ?

As I write, a memorandum is before me which has pursued me across years and continents. It asks me (after five years' absence) to fill in a form allocating my periods of service under Provincial Governments (with dates) the Central Civil Government (with dates) the Marine Department (with dates) the Railway Department (with dates) the Post and Telegraph Department (with dates) the Military Department (with dates) and to give the period of leave I took during the whole of my service " with nature of leave." A *babu* evolved this document in Lahore, and only another *babu* could answer it in London.

Similar conundrums arrive daily, by dozens, in every civil and military office in India. If tyranny exists in that country, the despots are those mild and well-meaning men who are snowing-under the administration with sheets of foolscap, smudgily typewritten and illegibly signed by Deputy-Assistant-Something-Or-Others. The *babus* write to each other. We sign their letters, scribbling away our birthright amidst mountainous files, and losing all touch with the people of India.

Every day I wrote away until two o'clock in the afternoon, with the Head Clerk at my elbow to see that I did not miss anything.

By dinner time, a new flood of paper was ready to engulf me. Accounts. Objection statements. Confidential documents. Secret papers in three envelopes, of which the innermost was sealed. And a pile of petitions which were not trivial only because they were human. A syce demanded ten days' holiday to Benares, in order to burn his mother, who had just died there.

Benares ! Why had I allowed five years to go by like a dream, a flash ?

Agra ! Sivanand ! During all this time, my conversation with the pundit had lain fallow in my mind. Sometimes it would bob up to the surface at odd, impossible moments, but more often it had remained unseen, an idea working in the dark. Fifty pleasures and duties and anticipations had kept me from the path that my inward eye had detected. Yet the inward eye sees more clearly than the frontal stereoscope. It sees what is good for us, as the compass needle points to the north.

I called for one of the beige papers on which applications for temporary leave were made out and signed my name at the bottom of the blank sheet.

" Please fill in this form for me," I told the Head Clerk, " and have it counter-signed by the Colonel, whose permission I am going to ask now, and then have it sent quickly to the Brigade."

" Yes, Sir. What is the time, place and purpose of the holiday ? "

" I am going to study the Kingly Wisdom and Kingly Mystery of the Unborn, Undying, Unbegun, *babu-ji*. I am going to Agra, and hope to return a wiser man."

" That will be ten days only, Sir, unless it is to cut into your privilege leave. Agra. Recreation. Very good, Sir."

Propped up on my sofa, I lay watching the delectable landscape that unrolled itself before the window of my train.

My future seemed clear. Here were the plains of

India, made for the pursuit of pig; and beyond them, the holy cities and the mountains. Between the two my life was to follow pleasant paths.

In the twilight that precedes the dawn, I was standing on the far bank of the Jumna at Agra, looking across river to the Taj Mahal. One should come to that light and lovely tomb as I approached it that morning, for then it will be seen as its builder intended, across a foreground of water.

I knew that if I did not find Sivanand Joshi here, I should find another. I was under sway of the sanctuary and the hour. I felt a rightness in the time and place—and a growing exaltation. Destiny had led me here: not eyes, nor ears, nor nose told me this, but the skin, through millions of avenues. My fate had been built up day by day out of a thousand actions and reactions. It was for this moment that I had waited and worked.

On the crescent that crowns the dome of Mumtaz's tomb, the heralds of the morning had come. Where I stood it was dark, but the dome had begun to glow like a pearl, like a monstrance above an altar. For me it was a symbol of the unity of worlds visible and invisible. One greater than Mumtaz was there, Unity itself.

The life I led as a soldier and this jubilant dawn were but the forms and guises of reality, the veils and vestures of ultimate truth. . . .

No one can describe the contact with Reality which is rapture, yet everyone, I suppose, experiences it at some moment of his life. The most we can do is to put down a few inadequate words that report not the thing itself, but a memory of light, and more light.

The sense-world slid away, and I sat no longer by the river, but by an ocean of bliss. It was a glimpse, a gathering-up, a heightening of the senses on every plane, not least the physical—an effulgence of eternity. I think that this was a turning point in my life : the sharpest turn.

Treading on air, in the freshness of that morning, I strolled along up the river, following my feet, and arrived at a rustic funeral. The relations must have been poor, or miserly, for the pyre was of green wood, and smouldered. But death has no terrors for the Monist ; and there was no sadness in that simple rite. For five thousand years the Hindus have faced the dissolution of the body in the lofty spirit of the Rig Veda :

Thine eyes shall seek the solar orb,
Thy life-breath to the wind shall fly,
Thy part ethereal to the sky,
Thine earthly part shall earth absorb.

Thy Unborn part shall Agni bright
With his benignant rays illume,
To guide thee through the trackless gloom
To yonder sphere of love and light.

Only the burners of the dead still lingered by the body. The next-of-kin had already sent the spirit to its home on the wings of the sacred *mantra*—" Go forth and follow the ancient paths our fathers trod." The flames burned low and like a witch's oils, and the scavengers of the Jumna—its crocodiles and tortoises and pariah-dogs—awaited all that remained from the pyre.

I walked on, and almost stumbled over a sack-like object huddled at my feet. It was dressed in Yogi's yellow, and was looking at the dark river—not across it to the Taj Mahal in the splendour of the risen sun—where the eddies of the Jumna swirled.

The figure turned, and looked up to me with a frank, unfaltering regard. I was puzzled as to its sex, for its face was powdered with wood ash, and its mouth gentle—a woman's rather than a man's. Ropes of black hair hung from its shoulders.

" Who are you ? " it asked softly and in a boy's voice.

" I am an officer in an Indian Cavalry Regiment," I answered, listening to what I was saying with some surprise.

" Why do you come here ? "

" Who are you ? " I asked.

" I am a *brahmacharin*[1] from Benares," he said. " My father is a *pandit* there. I read up to the Matric. exams. Then I became tired of this world and turned to the greater wisdom."

[1] Ascetic student.

So saying, he pulled out from under him a part of the deerskin on which he sat cross-legged, and motioned to me to take my place beside him.

I did so, wondering whether I had at last taken a jump out of my daily life, or whether I would be disappointed again.

" I would like to be a Yogi," I heard myself saying.

" Many men wish to follow the Way, but it is not for all."

" How can I find it ? "

" The journey is a long one, Sahib, even to initiation. If you find the path quickly, it is like finding money quickly—quickly lost again. So my *guru* says, and I am sure he is right, although I have never had any money to lose."

Was he a beggar ? I laid before him two silver rupees and a gold mohur.

He looked at the gold mohur doubtfully.

" With that I could take the train to Katgodam," he said, " and join my *guru*, who is going to the hills. But he told me to stay here another year."

" Does your *guru* always go to the hills and leave you in the plains ? " I asked.

" Yes, he goes every year. He teaches me for three months at Benares. The rest of the year I earn my living by begging. Take your gold mohur, Sahib. These two rupees will feed me for two weeks."

So saying, he put them into a small box, in which I noticed some Virginia cigarettes.

" So you smoke ? "

" A little. After *pranayama*[1], sometimes, or when the stomach is too empty for comfort."

I opened my case and offered him my cigarettes.

" I ate gram and drank milk last night," he said, " a big meal. And all night I slept here, so I am neither tired nor hungry now."

" And wanting nothing ? "

" Except wisdom," he answered, " and the man from the West. Perhaps you are he."

" Is your name Sivanand Joshi ? " I asked with a jump. " If so, I met your uncle at Delhi."

" I have an uncle at Delhi. But it was my *guru* who told me that an Englishman might come."

" Will you take me to him, then ? "

Sivanand looked at me with level eyes.

" Will you take me to Benares ? " I repeated, " or wherever your *guru* is ? We will go together. You said you would like to see him again."

" Katgodam is a threshold. Beyond it we cannot pass."

" Katgodam is a railway terminus," I said, " and from there we can go anywhere we like. Come, we will find your *guru*."

[1] Breathing exercises.

"Sahib, I will tell you a story," said Sivanand blandly, looking down to the river again. "When I first began to study the Science of Sciences at the lotus feet of my *guru*, I was always asking him how soon I could attain God-consciousness. So he told me of the *brahmacharin* who said that he desired *samadhi*[1] more than anything on earth. This *brahmacharin* and his *guru* were bathing at Gunga-ji at the time. Suddenly the *guru* took his pupil by the neck and plunged him under water. After a time he began to struggle and kick. The *guru* let him come up for a moment, just long enough for him to take one breath and to hear his teacher say that he would give him God-consciousness if he could bear it. Down he went again, and remained under water quietly, waiting for the Clear Light to shine. But blackness came, instead of the Clear Light. And as the *brahmacharin* could not find bliss by drowning he began to struggle violently and escaped from the *guru* and ran away. The *guru* went on bathing as if nothing had happened, and the *brahmacharin* waited for him, fearfully, on the bank. 'Do you still want God-consciousness?' the *guru* asked, when he had finished his prayers. The *brahmacharin* touched his master's feet and answered that he did. 'But what did you want most when you were under water?' asked the *guru*. 'Air,' said the pupil. 'Then you don't want bliss as much as breath,' the *guru* answered, and the *brahmacharin* had to

[1] That bliss which is knowledge of the One.

admit that that was the truth. So he was sent out, as I was, to seek wisdom by begging and meditation. When my first year was over, my *guru* taught me a little, and then sent me out into the world again. Five times this has happened, and I am not ready yet for the high and secret things which he will whisper to me when the time has come."

"How long will it be to your initiation?"

Sivanand shrugged his shoulders, without answering.

"I wonder," I said, "why your *guru* told you to wait here for a man from the West?"

"He did not tell me to wait here. But there is no difference between one place and another. You would have found me, wherever I happened to be."

"I was told, years ago, that you were in Agra."

"I have been to a hundred places since. If you had been ready, your mind would have led you to any one of them. Everything exists in Mind. That which men burn here was never diseased or dead: they offer up a sacrifice to that Becoming which is an aspect of the Godhead.[1] Existence-consciousness-bliss is never diseased, or dead, or burned, but always and for ever free from the conditions of *avidya*.[2] So to find one's *guru* is a simple matter, once the aspects of the sense-world are seen for what they are."

"I do not understand that."

"I shall tell you another story, Sahib. In the

[1] *Maya*. [2] Ignorance.

beginning of this Kali Yug[1] there were two *saddhus* in the Himalayas who discussed together how they could make themselves more comfortable on earth, for near their cave there were many rocks and thorns which cut their feet. One of them suggested killing a quantity of cows and tanning their hides and spreading them over all the earth as a carpet. The other *saddhu* considered this for a year. Then he said 'I have a better plan. Let us kill one cow only,' he said, 'and put its leather on the soles of our feet, instead of on the earth, so that wherever we walk there will be a carpet below us. These two were the first Yogis. There is no difference between one place and another, one woman and another, one religion and another, one *guru* and another. The differences are the veils of *maya*. You and I cling to them still. But when we are strong enough to know them for what they are, we shall rule our fate."

"And I shall find my *guru* ?"

"If you go to Benares, Sahib, you may find your *guru*. You may. I cannot tell. But I will give you his name, since I was told that you would come. It is Paramahansa Bhagawan Sri. Having humbled your heart and slain the desire of works, you may find him."

They were slow, dreamy words, spoken not to me, it seemed, but to the Jumna which was carrying down the white flowers and the yellow flowers that are the daily tribute of India to her gods and goddesses.

[1] The Iron Age.

Amongst these flowers rose an arm, as if waving a good-bye. It sank under the even waters, without sound or ripple, but the turtles had seen it and were coming from every direction, making tracks like the periscopes of submarines.

A big white turtle reached the body first, and worried it, and raised its obscene idiot's head with a ribbon of flesh in its mouth, snapping and gobbling. Others arrived. Soon there was a red foaming and scuffling where the body of a girl had been.

I turned away, but Sivanand did not flinch.

"*Sarvam Khalvidam Brahman,*" he said "—all this is indeed God."

Somewhere in the distance, a bugler sounded réveillé. Its notes drifted to me across the flower-strewn water, with its corpses, and turtles, and the reflection of the splendour that Shahjehan had made for the love of a woman.

CHAPTER IX

BENARES

Hysteria was close to Sivanand and all his world. These Yogis, it seemed to me, had the logic of lunatics. Was the everlasting solitary introversion of the Brahmins indeed more spiritual than the ethic of the beef-eating Briton?

The question kept recurring to me, both now and later, but the appraisal of differences and distinctions is a sterile pursuit, and I tried to put such thoughts out of my head. Whether or not the Brahmins were wiser than men of my own race, they had certainly an ancient culture whose exploration might fill my life and the lives of many others. It was an adventure, this blending of the creative impulse of the West with the traditions of the East, a new quest that might lead mankind to new Eldorados.

In Benares my search would begin. There I should discover the answers to my questions, if they were anywhere to be found. I would leave aside my mental note-book and my innate tendency to seek for analogies and comparisons. I would be a Hindu, in imagination at least, and walk the swarming streets not as a man of this century, but as a mediæval pilgrim to Canterbury, or as a child who had listened to Peter the Hermit.

Such was my intention. In Peshawar, some years ago, I had been a Pathan to all intents and purposes. But in Benares, as soon as I had settled myself there for a proper visit, I knew myself to be a stranger. I could not go back through the centuries : I could not view my surroundings with the eyes of indifference. Some reforming devil would up.

With a part of me I wanted to sweep out the twisted by-ways of the holy city, to disinfect its temples, rebuild the crumbling river-front, put fly-proof netting round every sweetmeat stall. Yet I knew that if a reformer were to attempt to do such things I should join in his execration, for then Benares would be herself no longer. The city fascinated me and repelled me, like Yoga, like India.

It was no good pretending the repulsion did not exist : Benares is an incarnation of the Hindu mind, full of shocks and surprises. You cannot view her through the eyes of the flesh, or if you do you will want to shut them. Her real life burns in the Unconscious.

Her outer life is passed in the temples and by the river. The temples are terrible, the river beautiful. In the temples there is a worship of fœtus-like figures. smeared with red, that lurk amidst the acrid corruption of milk and wilted flowers, and cattle-ordure, and bats and blood. Elephant-headed Ganesha is there, with her silver hands and feet ; and the discs representing the Regents of the Planets ; and serpent-girdled Kali ; and the blue-throated god himself, Siva, who swallowed the sins of the world that men may be immortal ; and the symbol of the sexes, united and complementary. These things the Brahmins will assure you—and it is true—are not idols. The true god is Brahm. For the rest, the world had worshipped always the same divinities under various names, symbolising Desire, the eternal driver.

I turned away from these squalid sanctuaries. Corruption stank in my nostrils, but my soul smelt something different. At the Durga Temple a headless goat twitched in its blood ; close by a peasant couple fed the baby monkeys with parched gram, and a little boy brought a piece of lemon peel to Vishnu's altar, in case the god was thirsty. Pigeons nested between the gold plates of the dome of the temple of Siva, and within, a cow munched the votive wreaths festooned round the *lingam* of the Lord of Names and Forms. These things were not meaningless, but their meaning came to me from far away, along pathways my brain had never used.

The river, on the other hand, was intelligible.

There is no sight more wonderful in all the world than the crescent-sweep of the Ganges on a bright morning, when Benares is at prayer. In that lustral rite, in which a hundred thousand people share, the squalor and superstitions of the streets are forgotten; we see here the ancient Aryans, still living in their descendants, glorying in sunlight and water, praying to God rather than to demons, untrammelled by the accretions of the centuries, and out of the clutch of their many-armed idols.

Three miles of crumbling palaces that lie in tumbled heaps with other palaces growing out of their ruins; and a confusion of richly-carved cupolas pushing their way between tamarind trees and tall flag-poles; and a fluttering of endless companies of pigeon among a forest of straw umbrellas; and below them a multitude of people who worship by the glittering water—peasants and priests, beggars and monstrosities and dwarfs, sacred bulls that have been married to four holy cows, cows with five legs, sleek girls with a skin of ivory and very poor and parched old women, fat merchants and thin fakirs, wise men and madmen, old and young, birds and beasts, all mingling on the bank and washing in the sacrosanct waters of the Mother—that is the river-front at Benares. The Ganges is so pure that you may drink beside her sewers, or amongst her corpses. She sprang from the feet of Vishnu, and from her was born the Hindu race. Her waters are jewels to the eyes of the living and a sanctification to the parted lips of the dead. Her cult is ageless and casteless.

The worshipper first offers flowers and rinses his mouth in her holy water. Then he kisses the earth she fructifies. Then, entering her, he worships the four points of the compass, raising his right hand three times, so that a trickle of diamonds drips down in homage to the risen sun, and whispering the oldest prayer known to man—the *Gayatri*—with which the Brahmins have greeted the Giver of Life for the mornings of five thousand years. Then he submerges himself completely in the Mother, rinses his loin-cloth, and returns to the river-steps.

In the temples, the cow's excreta is clean, but I am filthy. We creatures beyond the Brahmin pale may not touch a thousand objects in the city, but here, lovers of Gangi Mai, we are one people.

If I stood on my head at the Bathing Place of the Sacrifice of the Ten Horses, I should only be doing as a dozen others. Even less conspicuous should I be at the Scindia Ghat, which is the favourite of all the forty-seven bathing places of the city with the *brahmacharins* and ascetics of every cult, who come here to find a peace the world cannot give.

At the Scindia Ghat I am myself. Myself in skin and marrow. A sympathy reaches out across I know not what gulf of time and ancestry to unite me to these people. Some are insane, some have diverted their vitality into their burning eyes, so that they live only above the neck and not in thought as I understand it at present, but all have a goal before their eyes which is also my goal. They are fellow-travellers on a difficult journey, some madder than I, some stronger, and all freer, less tied to names and forms.

In another life I have practised these austerities. I have sat cross-legged, like that *brahmacharin*, with the sun in my half-closed eyes, restraining my breath. I have stood on one leg, like that stork-like youth, whose right foot is tucked into his groin. I have balanced on my head, like those two naked Yogis (as a child I was always looking at the earth inverted). I have been that girl, with caressing eyes. She is myself in another incarnation. Surely she will recognise her poor kinsman? She is sitting cross-legged, in *padmasana*, the ancient lotus-posture, with soles of the feet turned up and placed on the thighs. Buddha sat like that, and many before him. I also have locked my circulation at the femoral arteries listening, listening to the tide of all the world's vitality in my own body. She could, if she would, bring back that vanished time. But how shall I attract her attention? Is it polite to call her from *nirvana* to my foolish questions?

Near her, an old man is rolling over in the dust, holding a baby above him. Over and over he rolls, keeping the baby always in the air. Is the action symbolic of something? The baby finds the rotary motion agreeable and sucks its thumbs and smiles, but what kind of Yoga is this?

"What kind of Yoga is this?" I say out loud.

The girl draws a deep breath: it ripples upwards

under the ochre sheet that covers her, expanding first her stomach, then her ribs.

" He is going to the shrine of Kali, Sahib," she says.

" But why does he go like that ? "

She does not answer. Ought I to know ? Or doesn't she ?

" I have come here to find a *guru*."

" There are a thousand *gurus* in Benares."

" It is better to follow no saint than six."

" You know our proverbs : you also know then that a student may not reveal the name of his Master ? "

" I didn't know that. I am looking for a particular *guru*, named Bhagawan Sri."

" The Paramahansa ! " she exclaims, looking at me with velvety but passionless eyes. " He speaks English. I can take you to him, if you like. He lives on a pier by the house of Tulsi Das."

Shall I give her a rupee ? Yes, she will understand that it is a ceremonial offering. I touch the back of her right hand with the coin : she turns it up, extending her slim fingers without a word.

" Will you take me to him ? "

" Are you a missionary ? "

" Of course not. I am a student, like yourself."

She smiles a little, and her eyes assume a far-away look, beyond me, beyond Mother Ganges, beyond earth. Unless I keep silent she will help me not at all.

She is more incalculable than Sivanand, less sensitive perhaps, but more firmly centred.

Are we conversing subconsciously?

She uncurls her legs and rises, smoothly, like a yellow mist.

"Come," she says, "but slowly. I cannot walk fast."

Why cannot she walk fast? What rigours have crippled her limbs? Her body is lithe and young, but she stumbles, and walks like one in a dream.

On our way we meet a legless man, scrabbling in the dust with flippers six inches long, and nails growing in them, disconcertingly. He begs for alms and his gourd is empty. A rupee to him, to bring me luck. Here are three boys, squatting on a bed of spikes; and an ash-smeared creature, distorted out of human semblance, who is hanging head downwards over a fire; and a thin man, pulling in his navel so that it almost touches his backbone; and a crone loaded with chains, and another with a withered arm held aloft. How much masochism is here, how much fraud?

How many women Yogis are there? My guide shakes her head. Has she a *guru*? She will not answer. What sufferings has she undergone, and to what end? This girl is as baffling as Benares. Her eyes are lambent with love, but not for me. She will take me to the Paramahansa, but she absolutely refuses to give me any information.

I found the Sri sitting under a large umbrella, by a pier that projected from the house of the poet of the Ramayana. He was middle-aged, clean-shaven, bald, naked save for a loin-cloth and the sacred thread of the twice-born.

"I was expecting you, Sahib," he said joining his finger-tips in answer to my salutation, and bowing, "for Sivanand has written to me of you."

"You speak English perfectly," I said, sitting down beside him and feeling at home.

What could be more natural than the fruition of my hopes? For six years I had desired this meeting. Now it had happened. Time is nothing in India. *Karma* rules all, and the belief in its influence is infectious. I felt neither hurried, nor eager, nor surprised: this talk was planned before my birth: I had chosen the womb that should give me ears to hear it.

"Certainly I should know your language," said the Paramahansa, "because I have had every opportunity. But that is a long story and I expect you are in a hurry, like all Englishmen. I understand you want to be a Yogi. You know that there are two Europeans already studying with me?"

I had not known this, and it disconcerted me a little to find that the *guru* was reading my thoughts more exactly than I knew them myself. At the back of my mind had been the idea that I was doing something original.

" I am in no hurry, Sir," I answered. " I have waited six years since I met your *cheela,* when I was at Agra. He told me that I might come to you. As to being a Yogi, I am not sure whether I shall have either the time or the opportunity. I have come to ask you what Yoga is about."

" I am afraid I cannot say anything clever," said Bhagawan Sri, " like your Western lecturers. Moreover if I could show you a path straight and clear from your present world to the Brethren who live in the Himalayas—and I cannot do that—it would not help you at all, for at the ending of the road you would find nothing you had not brought with you. The Way is in your own heart. It exists only there."

" There is nothing, then, but imagination ? "

" From Brahma to a blade of grass, all is an aspect of Becoming. Brahm, not Brahma, is the only Truly-existent One, and it is profitless to discuss Him."

" Then what can be discussed ? "

" Everything except the Original Cause. If you study the Science of Sciences for a few years you will understand why. The laws of mental involution are no different from other laws : you cannot see the Mysteries with unquickened sight. You must not shut your eyes to the world, but rather develop the wings you have in order to flutter towards the Most High. I admit that a knowledge of the physical working of these wings is not absolutely necessary, but I and those that think with me believe it to be useful. Man has achieved bliss by a religion of rapture alone,[1] but the Way we follow is different. Instead of dragging the physical senses behind us like so much lumber, we ride them as beautiful steeds. The Clear Light of Reality may be seen by the mind, by the heart, and by the physical senses ; but mind and heart and body are never really apart. There is nothing but the Self. The body is an ant-heap of activities, living out their lives in its sun. To the lives within you, you are God, and these lives are God to principalities and powers invisible. They are in you and you are in them, for without them you could not live, as our God could not live without us."

"Amongst all these creatures," I said, "how can I pretend to be the One? In all this realm of knowledge how can I be the Knower? Above me as well as below me extend ranges of temperature and vibration that my consciousness cannot know. If I say there is nothing but the Self in the unimaginable worlds of space, then I am a solipsist."

"You have a name for everything," said Bhagawan Sri, "like our *pandits*. But a name does not give knowledge. Beyond thinking and imagination, there are subtler bodies which remain for ever outside mortal sense. Our Vedas said that, before your microscopes and telescopes. No one will ever see the world as it really is, even the greatest *guru*. *Samadhi* is but a rending

[1] The *guru* meant *samadhi* by the path of Bhakti Yog.

of one veil, when there are seven. It is an illusion, like everything else ; like your mathematics, which one day will prove to you that two and two do not make four. Such beliefs are useful illusions, necessary props. But *Sarvan Khalvidam Brahman* : outside Him not even solipsists exist."

" Some of our thinkers have already come to that conclusion," I replied, " but their methods seem to me to be more elastic, perhaps, than yours. They make all kinds of useful discoveries in the course of their researches into the properties of matter, such as electric light, which will surely make us all cleaner and wiser than we were. Are not such inventions more useful than centuries of inward-turning ? "

" Your methods are good in their way," admitted the *guru*, " but you are beglamoured by your achievements. Sheikh Abdulla Ansar of Herat used to tell his pupils, ' To fly in the air is no miracle, for the dirtiest flies can do it, to cross rivers without bridge or boat is no miracle, for a terrier can do the same ; but to help suffering hearts is a miracle performed by holy men.' You can turn day into night by electricity, but that does not give you more time to think. You can send messages over wires and so on, but such activities may be without discrimination. You have multiplied your bodies in enlarging your national *karma*, and produced suffering in proportion to your discoveries. England is full of monstrous phallic signs. You worship your factory chimneys. We also worship production, but knowing more of what we do. We worship it as the sign of renewal and as the Destroyer of Ignorance. We attend to the *rajasic* and *tamasic*[1] qualities of man. We deal with the three brains, the cerebral, abdominal and pelvic. We teach through the six principles of silence, listening, remembering, understanding, judgment, action. We consider the individual as composed of the five qualities of *akasha*, *vaya*, *agni*, *apas* and *prithivi*[2] and give him knowledge according to his needs, studying his subtlety, voice-pitch, vibrations, motions, respirations, smell and conversation. We study sound emanating from three places, the perinæum, the cardiac plexus and the mouth. All that exists is Sound in various shapes, but its highest vibration, the stillness of *samadhi*,[3] is only reached through *yama-niyamma*, *asana*, *mudra*, *pranayama*, *dharana*, *dhyana*.[4] By an illusory attribution of importance to these steps, followed by their withdrawal, as your mathematicians sometimes reason from a formula that is nothing but an abstraction and contrary to practical experience, we rise into God-consciousness. Then we knock the scaffolding away."

There was a twinkle in Bhagawan Sri's eyes. My impression was that he was talking to amuse himself.

"How, definitely," I said, "would you advise me to

[1] Practical and earthly.

[2] Roughly: ether, air, fire, water, earth.

[3] Bliss.

[4] Right emotions, postures, gestures, breath-control, sense-control mind-control and meditation.

start learning Yoga? Could I, for instance, begin by learning something about breath-control?"

"*Pranayama* would be more dangerous for you than polo, Sahib, for it cannot be performed without purification and prayer. The sleeping snake must not raise her head before her time."

Somewhere or other I had read that Yoga began with the internal purity, so I said that I was well aware of the necessity for making clean the inside as well as the outside of the cup and the platter.

Bhagawan Sri seemed pleased at my discernment, or glad to change the subject.

"You are right," he said, "my pupils wash everything, even their brains. *Mens sana in corpore sano* is a tag I was always using when I was a Headmaster. But you eat meat and indulge in an unnatural amount of exercise. The way will be long for you. Great forces are astir in the world, and you are living amongst these powers. They must work out their *karma*, even as you must work out yours, and we, ours."

Bhagawan Sri's pupils had returned for their evening lesson and were standing by the river steps, waiting to be called. Doves fluttered down from the palace ledges and flirted and bickered on the raft; a sacred bull stumbled down the steps and nosed the *guru*, as if wondering whether he was edible; and a fox terrier bitch appeared, brought by one of the pupils, wagging her tail and frisking round us.

"If I became a Yogi could I keep a dog?" I asked.

"Of course. Why not? She bathes with me every morning."

"In the holy Ganges?"

"The Mother washes her as she washes me. The Ganges loves all our India, rich and poor, man and beast. There is nothing she cannot purify. We give to her the bodies of our dead and we drink her waters. That surprises you, but even your test-tubes tell you that we are right, for if you analyse the Ganges water you will find that it is pure."

"That is because it runs over such wide stretches of sand and beneath so much sunlight, *guru-ji*. But I do not question your views," I hastened to add, "I only ask to learn them."

"Your feet have been led to the path. You have come here, and you will come again. To me, or to another, if I am dead. For you may not return for a long time."

Bhagawan Sri held out his hand.

I took it and rose, feeling that I might have over-stayed my welcome. He held my hand in both his, looking through me, rather than at me.

"Books will not show you Yoga," he said, "but life. You must live out your time as a soldier. I cannot tell when you will be ready for the path, but I know that you are not ready now, and that you will have to suffer more. I shall be sitting here under my umbrella for some years still."

"It is a privilege, *guru-ji*, to know that I may return. Already I feel something of your peace."

"When your breathing is equable," he answered, "you will have peace of mind whether you are being jostled in the market place, or are sitting alone on a black antelope-skin. May you travel the royal path and drink the fountain of its ending."

Benares was hung with mist when I left Bhagawan Sri, and the melon beds on the far side of the Ganges had grown dark. Down-river, a train was puffing over the red girder railway-bridge that my race has built in this city of abstractions.

Was all this talk of the Brahmins—the doubt rose in my mind like the tortoise I had seen in the Jumna—a screen to shield them from modern life? Or had they in truth a knowledge as dynamic as steam and steel?

A gong struck close to me, in contemptuous answer to my thought.

Men and women were surging into a temple doorway, an oil cresset fluttering over their glistening bodies. Inside, a throng pressed their foreheads to the floor, venerating the symbol of Siva, that had been anointed with rice and milk.

I looked back to the river, now empty of boats and streaked with reflected stars. Men and women were still praying on the steps of the Dasaswamadh Ghat and meditating there, for the Ganges is never without her worshippers. She greets them at dawn, attends them through the day, hears their vespers when she is crowned with stars, serene, aloof, apparently eternal.

A sacerdotal courtesan leant against the temple door, in profile to me, looking towards the river. Her nose tip-tilted, her upper lip lightly shadowed, her underlip a trifle projecting, her small breasts bold under her striped *sari*.

The *devadasi* and the Ganges : between them they received the outer worship of Benares. Other gods there were in stone and brass ; but those were dead, these the quick and adored priestesses.

Our railway-bridge and the minarets of the mosque of Aurungzeb dominated the city in a physical sense. But Christ and Mahomed had not prevailed ; and at Buddha Gaya, near by, where the Enlightened One first turned the Wheel of the Law two and a half millenniums ago, stood the ruined shrine of what was now a great foreign religion. Creeds and conquerors had left Hinduism untouched.

The *devadasi* glanced in my direction, and I drew nearer, looking into her so subtle and so carnal eyes. I expected—comprehension perhaps. But a conch bugled, and she turned her back on me, leaving me very much alone.

CHAPTER X

DEATH OF THE DEVIL

In the little world containing recruits to drill, ponies to ride, balls and targets to hit, papers to sign, Benares and its problems were soon overlaid by regimental duties, although not forgotten. One night when I was in the office late, struggling with secret mobilisation papers which I had to hand over to the officer replacing me before I went Home, the Woordie Major arrived to see me, all hot and bothered

Two crimes of an unusual sort had occurred, on which my advice was necessary. I had hoped to finish my work in time to catch the midnight train to Richa Road, for a last pigsticking meet at Ratmugri. But now I put my files away. One must be a patient listener if one would be an Adjutant of Bengal Lancers.

A pay sowar, the Woordie Major told me, had announced his intention of becoming a Christian. What was to be done with him? Obviously, said the Woordie Major, he could not stay in the regiment. We were Muhammedans. A clerk could be a Hindu and join other gods to God as much as he pleased, but not a combatant of the 17th Cavalry. Could I not reason with this misguided youth about his idolatrous desires? (Else he might get his throat cut, he added.)

No, I could not reason with him, I answered firmly. But it was desirable that he should go away and think over his conversion in a calmer atmosphere. Why not send him to the Regimental Farm by the night train? Extra clerks were needed at the Farm, and it was a thousand miles away. I scribbled a note to the apostate's Squadron Commander, explaining his sudden removal. A Christian, indeed!

The other difficulty had been caused by a spectre which appeared at the new ammunition guard. It had come at midnight, last night, and it had said to the sentry: "If you don't go away, I will come again with seven brothers bigger than myself, and kill you all." Whereupon the sentry went mad. He was Ghulam Haider, a plump Punjaubi whom I knew well, for he had recently been a recruit.

In what language, I asked, had it uttered its threat? Punjaubi, said the Woordie Major.

All day Ghulam Haider's friends had been holding him down to prevent him killing himself, or running amok. He had had several fits, and was growing worse. The Hospital Assistant could do nothing.

I sent for my bicycle.

First I went to the guard, and doubled it. Two sentries would certainly keep the ghost at bay.

Then to the hospital. Ghulam Haider turned the

sightless white of his eyes in my direction, and gibbered. When I touched his forehead, he yelled and threw himself on the floor in spite of the six sweating Punjaubis who were attending him.

Was it epilepsy? Why had the doctor not been sent for? As the Hospital Assistant did not answer, and seemed to have something on his mind, I took him aside and questioned him as to what was biting Ghulam Haider.

"He has seen something, Sahib," he replied—"but when the Doctor puts him in a straight waistcoat to-morrow, he will forget what he saw."

"We can do nothing?"

"What can we do? The world is full of illusions."

Yes; and I now remembered that the ammunition guard had been mounted for the first time only a week ago, when a sowar stole some nitro-glycerine from it in order to dynamite fish in a near-by stream. He was court-martialled and sentenced to imprisonment, but the finding of the Court was quashed because the ammunition had been left without proper supervision. So now the regiment had to find an extra guard, which was a nuisance to all concerned, and Ghulam Haider must have heard talk of this.

He was struggling like a man possessed, and screaming as if something was being torn inside him. Devils were working his muscles and using his lungs.

But it was not in my power to drive them out, and

Naim Shah was waiting outside the hospital with my dog-cart, to take me to the station.

Riding out to Ratmugri Bagh in the small hours of the morning, lulled by the steady swing of the camel and exalted by the close stars, I wondered what kind of Christ the pay-sowar had seen : had it been the God of the Sahibs, or the Mahdi of Islam, or some avatar of the Hindus ? And what was Ghulam Haider's ghost ? Could it be that through him the unspoken wishes of six hundred men were foaming out of one mouth ? Gods and devils were close to us in this climate.

We were all a little mad in India, a little touched by a sun that over-ripens men's thoughts. My pursuit of philosophy and pigs, for instance, was apparently illogical. Either I should devote myself to *ahimsa*, or else forget Benares and be a Bengal Lancer.

Yet reconcile these things I must, for I had need of both. Yoga was sound at core : its worships were those of a sane dawn, compared to the stuffy subtleties of the formalised religions of the West.

So with pigsticking : it sweated the false civilisation out of me.

Besides, the difference between spearing a boar and munching a lettuce leaf is essentially one of degree, not kind. An ox is big and bellows when slaughtered : a mosquito merely stops its buzzing. The mosquito wanted to feed on us, we on the ox. Who shall say that God intended the one and not the other, or that we may choose which of His creation we kill or cage or assimilate ? Every breath a man takes proclaims that life lives on other lives. We are all killers. Perhaps Nature represents the power of evil. If so, what a beautiful devil she can be !

As I swung along on my elastic-footed *untni*, the roses of morning gathered between the stars. It was that serene instant when day and dark are balanced.

No dawn is so swift and solemn as that on the plains of India. Other mornings may be tenderer, more mysterious, but none compare with these huge sunrises in rhythm. The dark plains stir, and wake, and grow radiant with promise : colours are massed and marshalled across the wide heavens, then swiftly, smoothly, light comes over the sleeping world. The rite is over and the miracle accomplished.

Surya reigned, and with his first rays I saw a big boar not two hundred yards away, following along the towpath of the Kundra Canal.

Spurring my camel and whacking her neck, I galloped into camp, and as she folded herself up by the breakfast table, I shouted the news to the coffee-drinkers. The Devil was ready saddled : I returned on him to show the way.

The boar had dodged into a patch of *arrah* ; as he

tried to slink out unobserved, he was viewed by a peasant, and chased into another crop, where we lost him.

Six of us had arrived by now. We rode back and forth, beating the cover with our spears.

At last the boar breaks again, taking us over the road-menders' pits, and across the canal : ahead lies a branch of the Ganges. The Devil slithers down a sand-bank and plunges with a snort of joy into the water. None of the others will face it : there's an ungentlemanly pleasure in that.

This boar is a very good swimmer. So is The Devil. I leave his head free, holding the cantle of the saddle and my spear in my right hand, and paddling with my legs and left arm. How delicious this cold water feels, through my clothes, down into my boots. With a squelch I am in saddle again, everything running and dripping. That's a stone handicap to our friend, but I'll catch him yet.

He's making for the *jhow* along the river-bank. Blind going, and I'm alone.

The Collector has crossed, but he's far behind. A long rein and easy seat—The Devil must stand up without my help. I can see nothing in this sea of *jhow* except the ridge of the boar's back. There's no skill in riding such a country : nothing avails but a good horse, and good luck.

I have no luck. Just as we clear the *jhow*, and I am gaining, green branches and white sand hit me in the face. The Devil has caught his foot in a twisted root, and fallen, but I have the reins. I'm out of the hunt. My fingers are a nasty yellow colour with the cold water. I wish I'd had some sleep and breakfast. The Collector is on the boar now, and another spear is riding wide, expecting a jink. The boar is winded. He'll charge. Yes, but the Collector's missed him.

I'll have one more ride on The Devil. Whoa, lad. That's better. I've soused down into the saddle, gathered the wet reins, and am off again. After this ride, it will be nine months before I feel the lift of his loins, and the snatch of his bridle as he judges the approach to a ditch. I need a rest. Indian earth is hard to fall on. I have swallowed much of it, too, and my loins ache. Am I growing old ?

No, by God not yet ! The boar's jinked again, away from the other spear and (oh, exultation incomparable !) towards me.

The Devil has the legs of the others, and of the boar. Steadily we draw nearer. There is no cover here, and the boar is blown.

We draw level. The boar's mouth is open—in another two lengths those big tusks of his will furrow the sand. He's charged. He's come up my spear. I can feel his breath on my hand. I've killed, I think, but why doesn't The Devil go on ?

Why *doesn't* The Devil go on ?

This riding, and fall, and riding again seems to have happened ages ago, but we are still on the same spot. The boar charged. I dropped my spear, didn't I ? Still The Devil is anchored, going up and down like a hobby horse.

My poor Devil—why didn't I guess ? When the boar turned over, a foot of spear entered your belly by the girth. Poor Devil.

Isn't that better now I'm off your back ? You are not dying, my friend ?

The Devil's forelegs were straddled and his proud head was sunk between them. He shook himself and lay down. He stretched himself out, as if he knew that the day's work was over. I staunched his wound with my handkerchief: immediately it became a sop of blood. He gave a little whinny, as if I had brought him corn.

Then his eyes glazed.

A stimulant might have saved him, if only Lashkman Piari with her medicine chest had been visible. The life was still there in him, but dammed up somehow in the sensitive nerves, so that the heart would not beat.

I waited by him, helpless. Kites circled above us. They knew. His life had gone out of my reach, leaving carrion where fleetness and fire had been an instant before. It was the suddenness of it that was horrible ; the knowledge that the ripple of his muscles and the swish of his tail and the pride of his eyes and the sweep of his stride were still close to me, although separated from reality by the time-lag of a nervous reflex. I sat still, not smoking, not thinking, growing gradually stony-hearted. Twilight came, and at last the elephants.

We hoisted The Devil on to Lashkman Piari's pad. Flies followed us back to camp.

I had no heart to continue pigsticking. There was a train back to Bareilly at mid-day.

Before mounting my camel, I asked that one of The Devil's hoofs should be cut off for me to keep (I am dipping my pen in it now) and that his body should be burned and scattered in the Ganges. Then, with the wail of his syce sounding in my ears I rode away from that good life for ever. After a few hours of jolted stupor in the train, I was back in the familiar round of cantonments.

CHAPTER XI

BEAUTY AND BOREDOM

In late May of this year, I was with my parents in a Castello on the Italian Riviera—and for the next five years my life was so far from its previous channels that I might have been on another earth.

Sometimes I heard from Bareilly, and learned of the remote happenings in the regiment.

The pay-sowar, I heard, had never intended to become a Christian at all, but had been a follower of a false Mahdi who lived in Quadian in the Punjaub. Since my departure, he had announced his readiness to confess to the faith of his fathers, and had duly repeated the *qualimah*[1] before the assembled Indian officers in the regimental mosque.

As to Ghulam Haider, who had been put in a strait-waistcoat as the Hospital Assistant had predicted, his return to sanity had been speedy. He had been passed fit for duty long before I had left Bareilly and I had ordered that a quart of goat's milk should be given to him daily, to fortify him against spectres. I now heard from the Woordie Major that he was becoming too fat for a cavalryman.

[1] The creed of Islam.

Brownstone and Daisy were doing well, as also were Maidstone, Tombstone, Judy, Jack, Whetstone, and the other puppies. To-day, their descendants encircle the Empire, but Brownstone and Daisy I never saw again, for they died before the end of the Great War. When I had patted them good-bye, I did not know for what far journeys we were all of us destined.

I heard also that Monarch, my young black Arab who was shaping to be one of the fastest ponies in India, had been bitten by a *krait*[1] while grazing, and was dead. . . . Yet here by the sapphire Mediterranean, Siva was incredible.

When the German Emperor entered the little blue bay of Portofino in the *Hohenzollern*, I dipped the Union Jack to him and watched his answering salute. He made a fine Imperial figure on his bridge, dressed in all the stars and orders of an Admiral, with the sunlight glinting on braid and jewels, and the withered arm well hidden. The fishermen of Portofino and I were much impressed. There was peace over that enchanted land and sea.

There was peace throughout that radiant May and June while I basked on the rocks, or lay in the bottom of my cat-boat, listening to her chuckling progress in a light breeze. And in London, in July, if there was not exactly peace, there was such a façade of pomp and pleasure that the war-clouds in Ulster and the Balkans

[1] *Bungarus cæruleus*, a poisonous steel-blue snake.

loomed only slightly larger to me than the Hunt Cup and the Eton and Harrow match.

How old I feel when I think of the opera, Ascot, Henley, Lord's, all the fashions and frivolities of 1914! When I had first left England, bicycling had only recently gone out of fashion. Now had arrived the era of motors which often ran for hundreds of miles without a breakdown; and aeroplanes which looped the loop. We seemed to be evolving towards a splendid Golden Age. In 1914, hostesses kept lists of young men of respectable antecedents whom they asked to their parties, and there was no limit to the number of invitations received by those whose names were on this register, provided they also had a healthy appetite for pleasure. I had, and was rarely in bed before dawn.

In that comfortable and well-ordered world, I took my small, but comfortable and well-ordered place. Future generations will envy mine, that has seen the rise of skirts from ankle to knee, and now their descent, with all that that implies. I feel that I am linked with the centuries in a way impossible to those born in this thin-faced, anxious age.

"It was great fun," I scribbled in a letter I wrote that summer. "On Monday I went to 'The Duke of Killiecrankie' with A's party, and then to a dance at Claridge's. On Tuesday to dine with A., and a dance at the Ritz. On Wednesday to dine with someone I don't know (introduced by someone I forget) and on to a dance. While there, Lady H. asked me to come on to the Centenary Ball, and with true American kindness she sent two tickets and two fancy dresses. So I went on with a friend to the Albert Hall. Such a sight. Lady Maud Warrender looked magnificent as Britannia, and when a suffragette came on to the dais and tried to make a scene, she only moved a little to one side to allow her to be removed. To-morrow I go to N. for Saturday to Monday. Next week I have to put on full dress uniform to bow at St. James's. There's great excitement over the Curragh business: no doubt Carson and F. E. Smith mean business, and some of the Navy will come over to our side. Then there'll be the deuce to pay."

Suffragettes and suppers, house-parties, a levee. . . . These things were blotted out of my mind by this friend with whom I went to the Albert Hall for the ball that celebrated a hundred years of peace between England and America.

She altered my view of life so profoundly that I never mentioned the change to anyone.

Yet to-day I cannot recall the details, except that she was dark and slight, and wore roses. We began to dance as soon as we were introduced, and went on for hours. Presently we were alone, at supper at a near-by hotel. All that I can remember is that her face flashed up in welcome out of a sea of faces, and was then lost to me in the storm that broke over the world. Except for this my mind is so blank about her that I suspect it of hiding something.

At the house in which I was staying in Ireland, a telegram arrived warning me to be ready to rejoin my regiment in India. Presently another telegram came, ordering me to a Cavalry Depot near Aldershot.

I went there in haste, hoping I was not too late to see the end of the War, and found "Kitchener's Kids" were pouring into barracks by the hundred. We had no saddles, but plenty of nice horses. The wounded from Mons had sad stories to tell.

The War was not over by September of that first year, and in September I landed in France, full of "cavalry spirit," and carrying with me one of the new thrusting swords, with which I hoped to transfix numerous Germans. A man, they said, died more easily than a pig.

"Here I am in a café in Havre," I wrote (then heavily deleted the word Havre), "drinking café-au-lait. I hope to catch the express to Paris, but may have to go in a troop train. The London Scottish came with me in the *City of Chester*. They are the finest lot of men I have ever seen in my life."

"The officers of the regiment I am with," I continued later, from the Aisne, "—never changed their clothes for three weeks during the retreat. We are billeted in a charming old farmhouse, resting. The country all round is beautiful. The guns continue without intermission, and lorry-loads of wounded prisoners pass. I am glad to be here, for we are sure to have lots of cavalry work. I rode out yesterday to see the battle. So far it has been in progress eight days. You can't think how interesting it all is. Please send me a pair of socks and some handkerchiefs every week."

Interesting. Lots of cavalry work. Socks. That is what I wrote.

We slept in our clothes, ready for a summons to lead the van of the pursuit ; lived on bully-beef, drank rum in our tea, read the English papers to hear how the War was going, re-organised, re-equipped. At dusk, each night, I climbed up to a plateau overlooking the Aisne, and watched and wondered. . . .

This was the war for which I had been trained, and for which I had trained my men, now thousands of miles away. A friend of mine (a Bengal Lancer) had killed two men in a charge during the retreat, and had been given a brevet Majority and a Croix-de-Guerre. Lucky devil. Here we hid our horses away. We gossiped and groused. Aeroplanes droned over us.

The battle was being fought in a tangle of little trenches, towards which I was not allowed to approach. When I attempted to do so, I encountered snubs and red-hatted Majors. " Soon the Allies will be again in full pursuit of a beaten enemy " ran a manifesto of Sir John French. As the days passed, we grew doubtful.

French reservists trailed into Soissons. " White mice " we called them, because they were small and humble. In the town square, rode Frenchmen of another type : brass-bellied troopers with horse-hair plumes in their helmets. The Cuirassiers sat splendidly on their horses, watching the white mice. We watched each other. Did anyone know what was happening? I was getting indigestion, that was certain.

Now in this part of France the cooking is the best in the world. It was absurd to be eating our rations when we might get a country girl to make us soup. I rode round ; seeking what we might devour. But neither eggs nor milk nor chickens were obtainable. "*Les Allemands ont tout pris—tout—tout !* "

The guns never paused. One night, alone in my field, I wept over the world. Heavy black clouds were massing upon the Aisne heights. Over there machine-guns chattered and chattered and chattered like the delirium of a giant hashish-smoker. All over Europe women wept, and the harvest lay unreaped. I wanted to scream, and coughed and cried into my handkerchief, much ashamed of myself. Was this lack of exercise, or too much bully-beef?

At last the suspense came to an end, and we rode northwards in great good spirits, for our division was apparently engaged in a flanking movement to take the Germans in rear. The weather was superb—and French girls were kind. . . .

" They give us fruit, wine, flowers, everything except cigarettes. I'm frightfully hungry in the mornings. To-day I breakfasted on a stick of chocolate, a cup of black coffee, a jug of café-au-lait, an apple and a pear, some pâté de dindon, a glass of wine and finally a cup of chocolate, all taken from the saddle. The marches are delightful as soon as the sun comes out. We get up in the dark, however, and it's cold then. Yesterday I had my first bath for a fortnight (in a pig trough). Beds are usually clean, but washing arrangements primitive. I have 'made' a good-looking German mare in a French farmhouse, where she was abandoned by the Allemands. I gave the farmer a receipt for her. She ought to be worth £100 after the show is over. A friend has just told me that an old lady in his last night's billet presented his regiment with a 50 h.p. limousine car. She wanted to give them another, but they had to refuse, as they only had one man to drive it. Every regiment keeps a car if it can—unofficially, of course. I want another pair of leather gloves, please, and a Jaeger cap to pull down over my ears. Also matches and cigarettes, as these can't be had for love or money."

I enjoyed myself until the day when we shelled the Mont des Cats, near Hazebrouck. In the evening, we bivouacked in the Trappist monastery on its summit. Our losses had been two officers and four men, but we had killed the same number of Germans. Our dead were laid out in a row.

My Bengal Lancer friend was one ; he lay there on the dirty straw, grey and limp, with a parson mumbling over him. I stood dazed, for he was a hero, and I could not believe that heroes ended like this.

During the night, my eyes would not shut, as if to make up for the days that they had been as blind as a puppy's.

We rode into Belgium next day and were greeted by the populace at Reninghelst with a barrel of beer. From there, I was sent forward from Messines with a patrol, to discover how far the retreating Germans had gone. Speed was vital. As I clattered along over the cobbles with my men, making noise enough to wake the dead, and expecting to run into a German rear-guard at any moment, I became very clearly aware of the fact that, " cavalry spirit " or no cavalry spirit, I did not want to die.

Here we were on the outskirts of Warneton. I had only to push on with sufficient bravery in order to meet an ambush. Some of my men would doubtless succeed in returning with the news that General Gough required, and one subaltern more or less didn't matter. But it mattered to me.

Stopping in front of a shuttered house, I roused the inhabitants, cross-questioned them, rode on cautiously, repeated the process, found the swollen corpse of a Uhlan. Gradually, we worked our way up to the crossing of the Deule, and halted there for a stirrup-cup.

The innkeeper came out unwillingly, but when he discovered that we were friends, and that I spoke French, he told me that the Germans were holding the opposite bank of the river. That was what I wanted to know. Several citizens confirmed his statement. I had just scribbled a message to Headquarters and sent it back at the gallop, when a violent fusillade broke out on my right and left. Both the other patrols had run into live, angry, invisible Germans. A loose horse galloped by, striking sparks on the stones. We caught it and trotted slowly back to Messines. For twenty-four hours we had been in touch with the enemy, but had only seen one, who smelt very badly, and seemed to me a good epitome of all this business.

I wrote out a full report, then lay dozing with my squadron in the market square. Presently word came that the General was pleased with our work. Well, if he was pleased, I was not, but I had at any rate learned a lesson not in the training manuals. I had grown much older and wiser in the last forty-eight hours.

All day I dozed. A spy was arrested in the square and collapsed in the gutter. Someone said : "He'll be shot at dawn if he doesn't die of funk before." Again I went to sleep. When I woke, I found a nun asking the men whether they thought that the girls at the Institution Royale would be raped if we retreated. I assured her that we were advancing, so that the question could not arise, and that anyway the War would be over by the spring.

But spring was a long way off. This was November.

We attacked a farm south of Messines, then retreated. We dug shallow trenches and left them. We cursed the plum jam. Our feet swelled with the sudden cold. Some of the men could hardly walk, but no one went sick. We became lousy. Lorry-loads and bus-loads of infantry kept streaming into the market square: cannon-fodder we said, and they were. It rained always. No one knew just where the enemy was, nor even, sometimes, which way we faced. Sometimes I was so sleepy that I wished that a bullet would let me go on lying down.

Then came a rumour. An Indian Cavalry Division was sailing for the front, and reinforcements of infantry. The more I thought over this prospect, the pleasanter it seemed, for the 17th Cavalry, who had been complimented on their military efficiency by every Inspector of Cavalry for the last five years, might well be chosen for service abroad.

My hopes came true, and I was ordered to report myself immediately to the Disembarkation Commandant at Marseilles, in order to take over the advance party of my regiment, which was due to arrive in France within a few days.

On my gay way through Paris, I bought a motor car

for the mess, and arranged for four excellent interpreters and a marvellous chef. We would seek death or glory with the best advice, and on full stomachs.

De-loused and shining-booted and a month-old veteran of the Great War, I sauntered down the quays of Marseilles to report myself to the authorities.

Here the blow fell.

"Your regiment? Didn't you know that you had a case of glanders at Bombay?" said a Staff Officer. "The 17th Cavalry isn't coming. I'm afraid we've nothing for you."

I shall pass over the next few weeks quickly—indeed the next few years—for when one is stunned one is not articulate, even in retrospect. And I remained orphaned, lost, rudderless for the remainder of the War, except for a few happy months in Mesopotamia.

Here I was alone and unwanted on the streets of Marseilles. The four wonderful interpreters would go to other regiments, the car would be re-sold, the cook waste his rum babas in the wilderness. Over a glass of light port in the Bodega, I considered the situation gloomily. I had nowhere to go. One place was like another to Sivanand at Agra, but that was small consolation to me in France.

Unpleasant as the fighting was, however, it could hardly be drearier than the line of communications.

In the Royal Flying Corps I had heard that there was adventure to be had without undue discomfort, so I decided to apply to be trained as a pilot, and to fill in the time meanwhile by becoming an interpreter to one of the Indian Cavalry regiments already in Europe.

Orleans was under snow when I arrived there as a French-English interpreter with the Indian contingent. We moved up the line with chilblains and coughs, and found Flanders under a sheet of white, with white trees against a pale blue sky. It was a beautiful, crisp Christmas.

Early in 1915 the weather changed. On a rainy afternoon a motor bicyclist came with orders from Brigade Headquarters and was away again in a flash. The news he brought spread from mouth to mouth.

The good lady who looked after my squadron insisted on preparing an early dinner for us, consisting of soup, cutlets, haricots.

"You do not know when you may eat again," she said. "Ah, *mon petit Fanou,*" she added to her pug, from whose nose I had been accustomed to induce electric sparks by rubbing him in front of the stove on frosty nights, "it is better to keep warm by the fire, you think, than to fight for France. *Hein?*"

Her only son was a very young *maréchal de logis*, whose photograph stood over the mantelpiece. When I rode that way again a month later, I heard from a villager that the boy had been wounded somewhere in Alsace, and that she had left hurriedly, hoping to see him, but that it had been too late, and that he was *mort pour la patrie*, and that Fanou had caught a chill and died also. I could not bring myself to face her, as I should have done.

We formed up on the Bethune road in the drizzling dark, our turbans heavy with the wet, and the men holding their lances in corpse-like hands. Our feet were frozen, too. Gulped cutlets lay heavy on my stomach; the hard-mouthed brute I rode kept stumbling. It was a most unpleasant march.

We walked on and on very slowly through the raw night, with star-shells going up in the middle distance and the voices of the guns growing louder. Ammunition dumps, camps, bivouacs, a mile of buses loomed up on the outskirts of Bethune. In the town we halted for a long time, picketed, moved again, picketed, yawned away to sit in a café, and then at dawn paraded once more, this time without our horses.

At last we were to see the Germans. Day broke as we formed single file to enter the communication trench. On and on we trudged, through deep mud, past coils of wire, field kitchens, field hospitals, gnomes with scrawny beards who were Royal Engineers before they took to the trenches. For an hour we plodded and twisted, then halted in a deep ditch. Bullets splashed between our loopholes, and sometimes through them.

We were in the marshes of Festubert, with the Germans eighty yards away.

In the trenches we smoked our pipes and drank our rum. Our men knew nothing about this Western quarrel, but it didn't seem very dangerous at first, and they preferred being active in a wet trench to lying night after night in a barn, in the verminous dark. As we neither attacked nor were attacked, our only discomforts were the wet and cold, neither of which were intolerable. Sniping and snipers kept us amused : the men were like children learning a new game.

A noise like a toy dog's bark came from a man in my section. On opening his shirt, only a small hole was discernible. Yet his lungs had been sucked out at the back of his tunic, and he was, of course, dead. We carried him back to the latrine trench, which was the only convenient place to put him at the moment, and here my foot sank in a soft place, and levered up a small brown leg, with toes splayed out. The Gurkhas had been there before us.

When night fell, I visited the dressing-station with a couple of wounded. Near the doctor's table, with all its ugly sights, was a ruined shrine in which stood a statue of the Virgin. Someone had written out these lines from Kipling and placed them at Her feet:

Mary, born of woman,
Remember, reach and save
The soul that goes to-morrow
Before the God who gave.

Cloak Thou our undeserving,
Make firm the shuddering breath
In silence and unswerving
To meet Thy lesser death.

Who had thought of doing this, I wondered? The verses belonged to another age.

The majority of us, of course, hoped for comfortable Blighty wounds. That was human. What was divine, was the bearing of those few whose souls rose above the battle and gave of their strength to others, so that bravery ran through the ranks like an electric current. All of us in the war saw such men, and the moments they inspired. For the sake of that, the rest was worth while.

Had I been killed during this time, it would have been only because I feared to be out of a fashion. Instead, I succumbed ingloriously to a fever. One doctor at Wimereux said it was appendicitis, another, bronchitis. Whatever it was, my temperature went down in a few weeks and I then became the willing prey of nurses in Mayfair. As soon as I could stand, I tottered to the Air Ministry.

A month or two later I was convalescent, and found myself strolling from Winchester back to my house at Twyford, across the lovely lawns of St. Cross and along the gurgling, glutted Itchen.

Spring had come at last. Those poor nuns at Messines would be having a hell of a time. We were luckier in England. And I became aware suddenly—as if a star-shell had glittered over my thoughts—of what the War meant to me. It was not a war for civilisation (which had twisted my mind out of shape) but for England.

My veins were proud that they carried English blood and that they were part of a stream greater than all present lives. I saw the careful fields, the opal distances, the lovely haze upon this land ; its sleek cattle, its sheep thick-nibbling the pastures, its rich content and strength. The physical sources of my being were revealed. I was nearly thirty, and learning to love my country.

Smile, reader, if you will. Your life may have always been passed in green places. Unless you have lived abroad you will have missed the comparisons that a returned wanderer may make ; as for me, I do not care how many may have expressed the same thoughts better ; nor would I exchange the memory of that afternoon for any other in my life.

It was raining. I looked down the churchyard of Twyford to the river, and across to the fields, and I thought of the energies that had gone into that soil to make it a garden, and of the blood that had been spent to keep it so. I was English, grown like the corn, like the grass, like the yew under which I sat, but not so useful or so ancient as the yew. England came to me like a goddess then, and I have held fast to her ever since, in a world where so much is so very uncertain.

CHAPTER XII

IN THE AIR

Outward bound, on the Red Sea, I looked across a little stretch of water, to where the hills of Arabia cut into the middle distance, and melted away into the retractant ranges of the horizon, nebulous and half-guessed. Flying-fish came up to play about us ; a shark showed its white belly, scavenging for tit-bits ; jelly-fish evaded us placidly, past our quivering side came creamy little patches of foam, and streaky patches, and hyaline patches that bubbled delightfully. I would have been content enough to be gliding on these agate waters, if only I had been going back to the front, instead of having been ordered to return to the 17th Cavalry, now a mere training depot in Allahabad.

I had not been at all the kind of man who was wanted in the Royal Flying Corps, apparently. Its doctors had tapped and tested me with an air of disapproval, and said nothing. Then my orders for India had arrived.

Over there in the glare, Arabs and Turks were fighting. From Damascus to Erzeroum, and from Beyrout to Basra, there were raids, marches, counter-marches, and insurrections. But I was being sent far from the great quarrel, to vegetate amongst recruits and young horses.

Sir Mark Sykes, who was a passenger on board, had been explaining the War to me. Turkey would be dismembered, he said. The Arabs were to have a kingdom; the Russians, Constantinople. If we won at Suvla Bay, where we were about to land a big force, the War would be over very soon. . . . Would it? I could not imagine peace in the East, now that the train was set. The life-breath of continents is longer than that of men, perhaps none of us alive would see the end of this unrest. But my path would be far from the blazes and explosions. . . .

I shut my eyes, for they were blinded with light, too much light.

But at Bombay, unbelievably, I learned that my destination was not Allahabad, after all, but Basra. I had been gazetted as an Observer of the Flying Corps and was posted to the recently formed Mesopotamian Flight.

Asking no more questions, lest this marvellous news should be contradicted, I sewed the coveted wings of an airman on my breast, and took ship for Basra, happy that I was still to be concerned with the two greatest adventures of mankind : war and flying.

On disembarking in the city of Sinbad (after having

puked through the Persian Gulf monsoon so that the deeps within me were as stirred as the deep without) I found a little bald-headed Brevet-Major of the Flying Corps, who was expecting not me but some aeroplane engines.

Had I brought the new Gnomes, he asked? Could I fly a Martinsyde Scout? How did they spot for artillery in France? Could I work a Goerz Graflex camera?

Well, I had had a Brownie for years, I answered cautiously. I could develop and print my own photographs. As to the Gnomes (should I say that they had been sea-sick?) I knew nothing about them.

"Why are you here?" asked Reilly, rather crossly.

"Because I've been sent."

"Haven't you got your ticket? Damn it all, I asked for a Martinsyde pilot and two mechanics and two Gnome engines—and all they send me is an Observer!"

"I'm sorry. D'you remember we were at Sandhurst together?"

"So we were. Have you ever flown in Caudrons?"

Now I had never even seen an aeroplane at close quarters, but I remembered someone saying over a cocktail in a château near Bethune (where I had once spent an evening with the R.F.C.) that Caudrons were disgusting buses, and that they threw oil all over the place. I repeated this observation.

"Especially in this climate," agreed my Flight

Commander, patting his polished head. " I don't quite know what we'll do with you," he added. " It's a disappointment. I suppose you can spot for the heavy batteries in the Farman Shorthorn ? "

" Yes," I answered firmly.

" Good. Two of us went west last week—forced landing amongst hostile Arabs—so we do want another Observer."

This is the morning of my first flight. Dust devils are swirling through the date-palms. The wind lifts sheets of sand off the Arab graveyard bordering the aerodrome, and the temperature is well over 100° Fahrenheit in the shade.

Start the " prop " ? Certainly.

" Look out ! You'll get your head chopped off ! "

Stupid ! I was trying to swing the propeller while standing underneath it. Here's a mechanic to help. I'll watch the way he does it.

" Contact ! " A heave and splutter of the engine. " Contact ! " The Maurice Farman is popping on most of her valves, slowly, fast, faster, now with a roar that rattles my teeth as I climb into the Observer's seat behind the pilot. What's this strap for ? To tie round me ? Well, we're off. Rumpety-bump. The ground slips away.

We've left it. We're sailing over the twisting Tigris. There's a cloud of yellow dust behind us. The leaves of my note-book are trying to tear themselves out in this wind.

Basra looks cool and beautiful amongst its green groves. A filthy hole it is on foot, but here the world is different. There are the marshes of Shaiba, where a battle has been fought : and up there, to the left of the river, near the old Garden of Eden, is the place where two of us had their throats cut by Arabs, the other day.

Revs, props, glides, pancakes, pockets, landing Ts, Longhorns, Shorthorns, Gnomes, Le Rhones ; all this talk is not impossible to learn by careful attention to its context. No one knows that I have never flown, and that until yesterday I had not the foggiest idea about even the theory of artillery observation from the air. It is really quite simple, however. I am to fire red, blue and white Very lights to indicate "short," "over" and "range." The battery has strips of cloth to indicate the direction of the target, and the orders of its commander : thus L means "observe for line," X "observe for range," E "repeat last signal."

Also I have made a list of everything required for the equipment of a dark-room. I have tested the Goerz Graflex.

I have learned the strength of Turkish battalions, brigades, divisions. I have been instructed in how to allow for mirages, count camels, distinguish between Arab and regular cavalry, calculate distance from gun-flash. Soldiering is far more interesting than I thought.

There's a cold wind blowing up my shorts. We have left the layer of hot lead that weighs on Basra. It's glorious up here. Has man ever known such bliss ? " To fly in the air is nothing wonderful," my *guru* said, " for even the dirtiest flies can do it." He was wrong. The world has found a new Yoga and will need new bodies before it can fulfil the possibilities of its last and greatest triumph.

Where's my Very pistol ? It's hard to find anything in this gale. The battery has just fired. That salvo fell short. Here's the pistol. A red cartridge. Simple. Now a white, for they have the range.

Ouch ! That was a bump, I suppose. I'll tell the pilot to circle to the right, towards the Persian frontier, to see if he really does what I tell him.

" Take O to R," I scribble in my note-book, and leaning forward, show it him.

He nods, and banks round so giddily that my inside jumps like a shot black-buck.

I am an Observer. Ten minutes ago I was an ignorant earthworm, but as Masefield says, " Life's an affair of instants, spun to years." I am lord now of another dimension ; the air is my hope and my love.

Damn ! The battery fired again, while I was writing to the pilot, and now we've swung round so that I can't see the result. What is the signal for " not observed " ? . . . Best do nothing.

The battery has now laid out an F on the ground—

not "fool," but "fresh target." Their shots have gone over : a blue light. Now short : a red light. Now short again : another red light. Now over : a blue light. I've ripped a finger-nail on this foul pistol. They have the range : a white light.

My pilot is scribbling in his note-book.

"Lot of oil on our tail," he passes back.

Is there ? What happens if you put oil on a Longhorn's tail ?

The pilot points downwards. I shrug my shoulders : he shrugs his : in this heat our engines are as temperamental as prima donnas. Yes, we may as well land before anything goes wrong. In fact, the quicker the better, for, being an Observer, I want to remain one until the next battle.

I shall like Reilly, and my work also. We live sensibly, without fuss or ceremony, in shorts, shirt-sleeves and sand-shoes. I have a good Flight Commander, and by all accounts a good General. "Alphonso," the troops call Sir Charles Townshend. He sings "The Spaniard who blighted my Life" and is a judge of champagne and of the dancing of the Gaiety chorus ; also a master-strategist. The men love him, and the Turks fear him, for he is lucky and victorious.

We are steaming up the Tigris now, in a red-hot iron tug with a drunken skipper.

We stick on sand-banks, are sniped by Arabs, drink a great deal of beer, eat, sleep and talk more than usual. The desert smells good at night : its stars are so marvellous that there is madness in them.

" Jumbo " Fulton and I (Jumbo is the nineteen-year-old pilot with whom I generally fly) share a stifling cabin. We discuss bomb sights, and how to cool the beer, and whether we shall take Baghdad, and what Sir Mark Sykes said, straight from the horse's mouth.

Before we reach Baghdad, however, we must defeat twelve thousand Turks who are entrenched in the marshes and canals guarding Kut.

Our tug anchors at Sunnayat, about fifteen miles from Kut, on the right bank of the Tigris. The photographic barge arrives next day, and for a fortnight I am flying, sketching, photographing, developing, printing, and pasting the result together into a pretty composite map—busier with responsible work than I have ever been before in my thirty years of life. The temperature still touches three figures in the shade. Sometimes I spoil a plate with my brow's sweat : sometimes our work does not finish till midnight, but we are always up at dawn to fly. Here at Sunnayat ten thousand of us are under canvas, with a couple of gun-boats, and half a dozen river steamers, and a dozen barges. Kut is twenty miles up-stream. Five miles from it, nearer us, at Es-sinn, the Turkish army is astride the Tigris, which here runs roughly west to east. Nur-ud-din's position is one of great strength. His right rests on a high irrigation cut, heavily entrenched and wired. A ferry connects this southern position with another system of trenches in the Horse-Shoe Marsh, north of the river. Then there are more trenches, another big marsh (the Suwada) and finally another mile of trenches more lightly fortified. Along this line, from south to north, Nur-ud-din is supposed to have five thousand regular and four thousand irregular troops, and eighteen guns. Another three thousand men are in reserve, nearer Kut, and on the Tigris he has six steamers, three launches, a dozen barges. The country is as flat as a pancake, except for the irrigation cuts and the marshes.

The Turks dig like moles. A frontal attack would be fatal in this open ground against such a difficult position.

Alphonso is full of confidence, however. He has telegraphed to Basra in his flippant way, to say that now that Nur-ud-din is within punching distance, he'll put him out for the count. We have pitched camp on the right bank of the river at Sunnayat, in order to make Nur-ud-din think that we mean to attack on that side, and we shall make a demonstration there, on the day before the battle. Then we shall march our whole force (or nearly all of it) across the river by night, and fall upon the Turkish left flank at the northernmost redoubt, which is mysteriously marked V.P. on my map.

V.P. That is the Vital Point, upon which Alphonso intends to deliver his main attack. I mustn't look at it too long when I'm in the air, or the Turks may guess our plans. One glance through my quivering binoculars is all that I may give it, then we bank over quickly and fly south, down the length of the Turkish position, with shrapnel bursting harmlessly below us.

The main force of the Turks is concentrating on the right bank of the Tigris. Here we circle round and round at our ease, counting camels, swooping down towards the square fort where we believe Nur-ud-din's advance headquarters to be, and occasionally dropping a few two-pound bombs to emphasise our presence and annoy the enemy.

We are safe, except for risk of engine failure, for there are no enemy aircraft. But two of us, in the only other Maurice Farman, have recently crashed in front of the Turkish trenches, and are now prisoners, leaving Jumbo and me and the Flight Commander as young gods on whom Fate depends. To us three, and only to us, the past, present and future of this country is spread out like a map each morning.

If only my eyesight were better, I should be happy.

But sometimes the responsibility of that morning glimpse of V.P. appals me. Are they putting up more barbed wire ? One line of it I have seen, compared with three lines farther south, and some ugly-looking pits, with stakes in them. Land mines also. And gun emplacements. I had hoped to show Alphonso a photograph of artillery positions this morning, but there was no ice for my developer, and the tepid metolhydroquinone curled the film off my plate. That may cost the lives of soldiers.

The great day has come : dawn of the 28th of September, 1915.

Yesterday afternoon, Alphonso made a feint attack on the Turkish right. Now he has transferred his whole force to the north of the Tigris, except two weak battalions. Eight thousand men have been marching through this stifling night to attack V.P. The remainder —a brigade of infantry—are to make a holding attack near Horse-Shoe Marsh at the Turkish centre.

If we succeed in this manœuvre—one of the boldest in history, for we have left only a thousand men to guard all our transport—we shall capture all the Turkish army in these parts, and enter Baghdad within a week.

We soar up over the black scrub of Nakhailat, and

pass over the pale, pink face of the desert. Our men are still marching, marching down there ; the Turks waiting and wondering. This time we shall see V.P. as it really is. The Suwada marsh looms up ; round it is a yellow mist. Now I can discern the blur of trenches where soon a multitude will die.

The stars vanish : a red sun rises : the guns speak. Here are my scribblings to Jumbo during a tense hour: they have survived the War, and I like to remember these snatches of talk.

"7.5. Hell of a bombardment in centre section. In front of Delamain. Our troops advancing.

"Down the front line to give them hell.

"7.25. Body of troops retiring D.3.3.5 behind Turkish trenches. Not a soul in reserve line.

"Cavalry moving out from Kut. Where is ours?

"Down to Delamain. There's the landing T.

"8.10. Can't waste time. This looks as if we'd won."

We have won. V.P. has been taken.

Shells fall round us where we land amongst some of our dead. As I run up to the headquarters of the attacking column, I see boys of the Dorsets and Oxfords, and men from the Punjaub, from Central India, from Madras, lying still, spread-eagled. The wounded are being carried back in stretchers. A batch of Turkish prisoners is being marched to the rear, begging for water. There is no water that is not brackish in these marshes.

Suppose we lost this battle? I don't know why the

idea flashes into my mind in the moment of victory. But it does. Is this a dream? What are we all doing? I drop into a walk as I reach General Delamain, near the taken trenches.

He is white with sweat and salt. A night march is always anxious, and three-quarters of his force is lost, for six battalions have marched round the wrong side of Ataba Marsh, to the north of us. It was half-past seven before he discovered this, but nothing daunted, he attacked with his remaining two battalions. It is a miracle that V.P. is in our hands. To gain it we have lost seven hundred killed and wounded, but the key of the Turkish position is in our hands.

Now we are sweeping round to attack the centre of this northern section, where the Turks are more deeply entrenched. With luck we shall take them in rear, but the absence of six thousand men makes the issue uncertain.

Bits of arms and legs are lying at the lip of the trenches. Our gunners had the range to a nicety. Yes, there was only one line of wire. My eyes eat up the features of this ground that I have been scanning for three weeks from the air. There were three gun emplacements instead of two—that was a mistake of mine. Most of our losses occurred when our men were enfiladed from the centre of the position, but the air report was right enough in saying that V.P. was weakly held in comparison to the other trenches. I must hurry back to Alphonso with this good-but-might-be-better-news.

When I reach Jumbo again, I remember that I have a full water-bottle at my belt, iced by flying, which I forgot to give to Delamain. Someone must have it. There's an old Turkish sergeant groaning in his beard and holding his stomach. He sluices its contents down his throat, looks at me in grateful wonder, gasps, falls down. Water is said to be fatal on a wounded stomach. Have I killed him by mistake?

Off we go. Alphonso is breakfasting in a kind of water-tower, from which he hopes to survey the battle as soon as the sun rises higher. He will see nothing, I know, but mirages; still, he must do something, and this dallying with eggs and bacon serves its purpose. His Sam Browne belt is stuffed full of revolver cartridges: he is resplendent, calm, confident. Napoleon has committed his veterans: victory will light on his eagles. The Staff seem grave (we have three hundred miles of desert behind us in case of retreat and only a handful of men to guard our communications) but not Alphonso. I tell him that V.P. is taken, that we have had heavy losses, that three-quarters of our force has gone astray.

"That's quite all right," he answers. "Fly back, and tell General Delamain that I am very pleased with him."

Not a word about the lost six battalions. I suppose

he supposes they'll turn up. Anyway, he is quite sure we'll win.

It is past ten o'clock when we return to Delamain, and deliver Alphonso's message. The lost battalions have been sighted, having plodded round the Ataba Marsh in time to join in the battle for the centre trenches.

It is lucky we have them. Delamain has not yet been able to dislodge the strong-kneed Turks, and our men are exhausted with marching and fighting and thirst. Some of them—Punjaubis—creep under our wings while we are reporting to Delamain. They should be fighting. Having had plenty of water and sleep myself, I have also some courage, but I am afraid of their fear, and am delighted when we are ordered to go up again into the fresh air.

Things are not going too well, as seen from above. Enemy reinforcements are hurrying across the river in support of their comrades, and the *Mejidieh* (a Turkish transport) is steaming down from Kut, laden with troops. All round the marshes mounted Arabs are massing. It is curious being up here, cool and safe, watching the ships and horses and men that crawl below us among puffs of smoke. I am the first man, and I daresay the last, to see the whole of an old-fashioned encounter battle from the air.

There is no sign of our cavalry, who are supposed to be striking terror into the Turkish rear. In front of

Horse-Shoe Marsh a battle is in progress. We cannot break that line with two weak battalions. Will the Turks counter-attack?

It is eleven o'clock when we return to Delamain. He has been able to capture but very little more of the enemy line, and looks ten years older than when I saw him at dawn.

Where is our damned cavalry? Nobody knows. I can't find out. The Turks are massing steadily.

The decisive moment that occurs in every engagement has arrived. "We'll take those trenches before noon," says Delamain: "The Oxfords are going to attack. I'll be with them. You two go up at once and report what's happening: it's now or never."

I salute, and run back to Jumbo who is standing by the aeroplane. As we take off, I see Delamain on a gun limber with field-glasses to his eyes, a tall, gaunt man, with jaw set: inspiration incarnate.

"At 'em," I scribble. "We'll chance the height."

A forest of rifles is pointing at us from the centre trenches, but the Turks will have no time to think of aeroplanes when the Oxfords get amongst them with cold steel.

Our troops have deployed and are advancing steadily, wave after wave of gallant men marching through the Turkish fire as if they were on a King's parade. Wonderful. The first wave has reached the trenches. Never shall I see such things again. A volley has burst through our fuselage.

Jumbo is hit in the neck ! Yet he's flying as if nothing had happened, with a red trickle at his nape. I must tie him up. Where's that first field dressing ? Fool that I am, I've let it stream back into the propeller. But we have dived out of rifle range. I lean forward and shout in his ear.

" What ? "

" Your *neck* ! "

He is too young to die.

Jumbo puts his hand up and is amazed at the sight of blood. He circles round once more. The opposing forces look like ants, tapping each other with their feelers. Some of the ants lie still. Hurrah, the Turks are leaving their trenches and the Oxfords are bayoneting them as they run !

" Down ! " I signal.

We must give the news of victory to Delamain. Jumbo makes perfect landing.

" Go to the ambulance while I report."

" Bosh ! " says Jumbo, or words to that effect.

There is no time to argue.

When I return, he is munching a stick of emergency chocolate. He has tied up his neck with his handkerchief and refuses to report himself as wounded, lest the doctor should forbid him to fly. It is only a scratch, he says.

The Oxfords have won the main trenches. We are still far from water, and have had more losses, but we have captured eight guns, and many prisoners. Delamain is so tired that he can hardly talk.

When we return to headquarters, Alphonso has come down from his watch-tower and is preparing for pursuit.

" The enemy will retreat," he says, " and I don't want them to escape in the night."

Is he as sure as he looks ? Yes, in spite of the fact that we have lost as many men as the Turks, that our forces are about equal, and that we have been marching all night and half the day under a blazing sun, while they have been sitting still, we shall win, for there is a strength upon Delamain and Alphonso.

Delamain is advancing towards the river now, and he may cut off the Turks by getting between them and Kut. On the other hand, he may not reach the river at all, for five thousand men and four Krupp guns of Nur-ud-din's force from the right bank are now crossing the Tigris by the boat bridge, and are about to attack his flank. From the air I see this clearly, but I can't tell Delamain, for there is no landing-ground where he is. We must try to drop a message.

I write it and drop it with a streamer attached. Then we follow up the Tigris to Kut, looking for our cavalry, and for signs of a general retreat on the part of the Turks. We keep at 4,000 feet—for Jumbo's neck is precious to the 6th Division—and scatter some of our bombs round the *Mejidieh*, trying to drop them down her funnel.

After an hour's flying, we circle back and land by Delamain at the Tigris. It is now a little after five o'clock, and he has won another battle. He saw the Turkish reserves in time, turned on them like a tiger, drove them back. But the men are too exhausted to pursue, having only just strength enough to drag themselves to the river, and drink, and be sick, and drink again.

Our own and the enemy wounded are being evacuated in barges. They are mad with wounds and thirst: the few doctors are almost helpless: it is a really frightful scene: poor devils creep to the dressing-stations on their hands and knees, over decks slippery with blood and diarrhœa.

We can't reach Kut to-night.

Once again we go up in the twilight. Jumbo tosses the old Maurice Farman about like a tumbler pigeon, partly because we've won, and partly because we must forget what we've seen. Groups of the enemy near Kut have clustered themselves together against the Arab bands that skirmish closer and closer in the gathering darkness, hungry for loot. At A.5.15; A.5.1.6.7.8., there are groups of deserters on the Baghdad road. I am busy with map and note-book.

At nine o'clock, in the dark, we land at Nakhailat. Alphonso has already embarked. His Staff have the figures of the Turkish losses : 17 guns, 1,289 prisoners, 1,700 killed and wounded. Our casualties are 1,229 killed and wounded. That's a fine victory.

For seventeen hours, Jumbo and I have been at full stretch, and for ten of them Jumbo has been in pain. Into them have gone anxiety, hope, fear, horror and joy, pressed down and brimming over. He and I and Reilly say little over our tinned mutton and coffee ; and my eyes begin to close before the food is finished.

CHAPTER XIII

THE LONG DESCENT OF WASTED DAYS

The pursuit from Es-sinn failed because our barges stuck on the sandbanks of the always-treacherous Tigris. At Ctesiphon the Turks rallied. Our main body halted at Azizieh, a dusty little camp some eighty miles from Baghdad and thirty from the Turks.

For a couple of months, during the lull in the fighting, I continued my routine between the desert and the dark-room. But by the beginning of November, 1915, it was apparent that a change in our mode of life was impending. Clear-the-line messages had been throbbing over the wires. Unit Commanders had met Alphonso in high conclave. To advance, or not to advance? Something had to be done quickly, for reinforcements were arriving for the Turks as a consequence of our fiasco in the Dardenelles. We had to go back or forward. So Alphonso made the best of what he privately considered to be a wrong decision, and recalled every available detachment from his lines of communication to prepare for the attack. Before the battle, he had convinced us all that the Mesopotamian capital was within our grasp.

Meanwhile, an Australian pilot and I were chosen to cut the telegraph lines that run east and north of Baghdad, in order to isolate the city from the troops hastening southwards under Marshal von der Goltz. The round trip would be two hundred miles, at least, and as our machine could only keep the air for three hours without refuelling it was necessary to take spare petrol and oil, and fill up before returning.

After dinner on the eve of this adventure, I spent an hour with the engineers, testing detonators, and primers, and slabs of gun-cotton. I turned-in early and slept well, confident of success. We would have to land twice in hostile territory and make two demolitions; but I never doubted that all would go well.

Already I looked forward to a holiday after the capture of Baghdad. I had been promised a transfer to the training-school at Cranwell as soon as I could be spared; and I told myself now that I would return with a new ribbon under my wings, and a Persian carpet in my luggage.

Before dawn on November 13th "Australia" White and I stowed away eight extra gallons of petrol and four of oil in the old Maurice Farman.

Up we went into the still air, away from our sleeping camp. The bivouac fires of the nearest Turkish outpost at El Kutunie mounted straight to heaven. It was a clear morning.

A few of the enemy were bustling about, and rubbing their eyes, and cursing us, for we had disturbed them earlier than usual. Away to the south, one of our steamers was threading her way up the shoals of the

Tigris, carrying reinforcements and the English mail. I told myself that I would find good reading on my return, and have good news to write.

Down there the world was still in a velvety purple twilight, but our fuselage was spangled with light from over the Persian hills. Ahead there was Zeur, the chief Turkish outpost, with its twenty-times-snapshotted trenches. Now the sun had begun to slant across the scarred face of the desert, showing up men and horses and mounds and irrigation cuts in strong relief.

The enemy had been active since last I had viewed his dispositions, forty-eight hours ago. In the maze of trenches by Seleucia there were more zigzags than ever. Grass huts were building by the Arch. Six barges were being towed down from Qusaibah to the main position, gravid with troops. A thousand camels carried provisions towards the new " V.P." A convoy drawn by white horses looked German in its glinting precision. There would be much to tell Alphonso, when we returned. I longed to study these preparations better, but that would have to wait until to-morrow—perhaps.

Perhaps? No, certainly to-morrow. Wire-clippers hung at my belt, and pencils of fulminate of mercury reposed in my coat-pocket, out of harm's way but readily accessible. The brown road leading from Baghdad to Feluja stood up out of the surrounding pinkness. That was our objective, for the telegraph lines ran parallel to it, but near Baghdad I saw that there was a constant traffic of horsemen and camels. We would have to fly west, into the desert.

We turned away from Baghdad, looking immense and magical under its date-palms, and headed towards the Euphrates glimmering on the horizon. The two rivers, the five lakes, the city and the mountains, and far to the north the gold domes of Kazimain, were sights to fill the eyes, had it not been for the nearer view of five or six thousand camels, swaying and slouching towards the markets of the capital. Those brutes were a blot on the landscape.

I felt as if I were at the start of a race, watching for the gate to rise.

We circled down towards the most solitary part of the line visible to us, at a place called Nimrod's Tomb. In two minutes we would know our fate.

The next two years, however, I would like to pass over without comment, for they are a time apart in my life. But as I cannot leave the reader in mid-air, I shall repeat what I have already written in order to bring this exploit to its end.

" We made a perfect landing and ran straight and evenly towards the telegraph posts. I stooped down to take a necklace of gun-cotton from the floor of the bus, and as I did so, I felt a slight bump and a slight splintering of wood.

" We had stopped.

" I jumped out of the machine, still sure that all was well. And then——

" Then I saw that our left wing-tip had crashed into a telegraph post. Even so, the full extent of our disaster dawned slowly on me. I could not believe that we had broken something vital. Yet the pilot was sure.

" The leading edge of the 'plane was broken. Our flying days were finished. It had been my pilot's misfortune far more than his fault that we had crashed. The unexpected smoothness of the landing-ground and a rear wind that no one could have foreseen had brought about disaster. Nothing could be done. Nothing remained—except to do our job.

" I ran across to another telegraph post, leaving the pilot to ascertain whether by some miracle we might not manage to taxi back to safety in our running partridge of a machine.

" By the time I had fixed the explosive necklace round the post, a few stray Arabs, who had been watching our descent, began firing at us from horseback. I set the fuse and lit it, then strolled back to the bus, where the pilot confirmed my worst fears.

" Presently there was a loud bang. The charge had done its work and the post was cut neatly in two.

" Horsemen were now appearing from the four quarters of the desert. On hearing the explosion, the mounted men instantly wheeled about and galloped off in the opposite direction, while those on foot took cover, lying flat. To encourage the belief in our aggressive force, the pilot stood on the seat of the bus and treated them to several bursts of rapid fire.

" Meanwhile, I took another necklace of gun-cotton and returned to my demolition. This second charge I affixed to the wires and insulators of the fallen post, so as to render repair more difficult. While I was thus engaged, I noticed that spurts of sand were kicking up all about me. The fire had increased in accuracy and intensity. So accurate, indeed, had it become, that I guessed that the Arabs (who never can hit a haystack) had been reinforced by regular troops.

" I lit the second fuse, then covered the hundred yards back to the machine in my best time, to reach cover and companionship. A heavy fusillade was now being directed on to the machine, at ranges varying from fifty to five hundred yards.

" Bang !

" The second charge had exploded. The telegraph wires whipped back and festooned themselves round our machine. The insulators were dust.

" Doubtless the damage would take some days to repair : so far so good."

The rest was bad. Our captors were Shammar Arabs, who debated among themselves whether to cut off our heads, or whether to bring us living to the Turkish Commander at Suleiman Pak and claim a modest reward for our capture. Fortunately for us, a detachment of Turkish mounted police arrived while this discussion was in progress, and decided our fate by taking us from the Arabs. We were borne in triumph into Baghdad, where the populace spat in our faces.

Then, while the British attack at Ctesiphon was at its height, we were sent north to Mosul, and imprisoned in the fortress there. So we passed out of the world of living men, into prison life.

The truth about the next twenty-four months it would not be in my power to write, even if I wished to do so. And I do not wish. Prisoners see war without its glamour. The courage and comradeship of battle is far from them. They meet cruel men, and their own fibre coarsens. A chronicle of these wasted and miserable hours, of dirt and drunkenness, of savagery and stupidity, would not only be dull, but remote from my subject.

I shall record only two incidents therefore : to write more would be useless, to write less would be to forget that out of fourteen thousand prisoners of war in Turkey only some three thousand returned to England.

I saw a party of twenty English soldiers, who had been marched from Kirkuk across the mountains, arriving moribund on the barrack square at Mosul. They were literally skeletons alive, and they brought with them three skeletons dead. One of the living men kept making piteous signs to his mouth with a stump of an arm in which maggots crawled. Presently he died in a fit.

Then there was the saddest tea-party at which I have ever assisted. We had bribed a sentry to allow us to give two of these men a meal of bread and buffalo-cream which we had prepared out of our slender resources. Our guests told us that they were kept in a cellar, with hardly enough room to lie down. Only drinking water and bread were supplied to them. They could not wash. Three times a day they were allowed to go to the latrines, and sometimes not then, for if a prisoner possessed anything that the sentry wanted, he was not allowed to go until he had parted with it.

One of the men now fainted. The other explained that, starving as they were, our fare was too rich. "Australia" White, who was always foremost in kind offices, carried the sick man on his back to the cellar, past the bribed sentry, and attended to him as long as he dared. But it was to no avail. When he returned, his clothes were swarming with vermin, for lice leave the dying.

When our pay was given us, and an opportunity occurred to bribe the guards, it was a heart-breaking business to decide which of the sufferers we should attempt to save. Some were too far gone to help, others might manage to live without our smuggled food. But it was little enough we could do before we were transferred to Aleppo, and thence to Afion-Kara-hissar, " the black opium city " in the centre of Anatolia.

The soldier survivors followed. Many were clubbed to death by the sentries and stripped naked. Others, more fortunate, were found dead by their companions after the night's halt, when they turned out to face another day of misery.

A criminal's sentence is fixed, but not that of a prisoner of war. Settled in Afion-Kara-hissar, the future seemed an endless avenue, leading nowhere. Spring came, and the days succeeded each other in a pageant in which we had no part, cooped up as we were. I know now why drunkards drink, and how caged canaries feel, and all about bugs. Lice we are all familiar with, who served in the War. Fleas are lively little beasts. Scorpions, hornets, wasps, mosquitoes, leeches have none of them the Satanic quality of bugs.

One squashes a bug and there is a smear of blood—one's own blood. One lights a candle, and there, scuttling under the pillow, are five or six more of the flat fiends. Having killed every living thing in sight, one lies back, hoping to sleep. But they smell horribly when dead, and keep alive the memory of their itching at neck and wrist. Presently out of the corner of one's eye one sees monsters darting about avidly, magnified and distorted by proximity. There is no end to them. You kill them on the bed and they jump on you from the walls. You slaughter them by fives and tens, but still they come from the crannies where they have lain for months—years maybe—waiting for the scent of live bodies. They batten on the young : of two victims they will choose the healthiest. They not only suck your blood, but sap your faith in God.

Under these circumstances, I took to Yoga. It was little enough that the *guru* had told me, yet that little, with some books I had read, and the immense leisure of these days, enabled me to practise certain writhings and breathings which I should not have attempted during an active life. Time is the essence of Yoga. The exercises must be repeated until they become a habit. At first I was inclined to be sceptical of results, then surprising things began to happen.

The " head-stand " was a mild gymnastic which I had learned at Sandhurst. Performed according to Yogic directions, however, it did seem to wash my brain. I felt a little giddiness, a slight ache in the jaws sometimes, but also distinct pleasure in a position which my ancestral relatives must often have adopted. Sixteen hours a day of uprightness is unnatural for the human inside : it is good for it to hang occasionally the other way up.

Then I tried a breathing exercise. My early sensations were of dizziness, but soon there came a kind of clearing in throat and eyes and ears and brain. My heart at first accelerated and then retarded its beat. After three spells of twenty-one breaths each, I tried another group of breathings, quicker this time, until I became drunken with oxygen and rolled about and laughed.

But I might as well try to describe a trip to the moon as tell of such confrontations of the body with its Self.

Poised and relaxed and completely in my body (not out of it, as the mystologues would have it) I saw myself at times impersonally. The future lay at my feet. I surveyed it as an interested traveller, knowing that in some parts of it I could never live, with my volatile brain ; and that in others I was destined to be useful. I seemed to stop breathing then, as one gasps at some beauty suddenly revealed, but this arrest of the heart (if it was that) was smooth and delicious, a sliding into peace.

And I began to realise, with awe, a millionth part of the temptation in the wilderness. When Christ saw the kingdoms of the world before Him, He may have known, in an unimaginably vivider degree, such a clearing of the mists of the desire-mind as I had experienced. His temptation may have been a choice of paths.

In my enthusiasm, I practised the *bhastrika* strenuously. Again and again I tried it, sending my pulse up to 110, 130, 140 and more. Might not the telescope of of the lungs reveal the star of Christ? One night my finger-tips became blue, and I could not sleep. When I experimented with the head-stand next day, in order to whip-up my circulation, I fainted.

So I tried the writhing *mudra*. This gentle grinding of the inside so stirs the thermostatic arrangements that the student of Yoga begins to perspire freely, and with that opening of the pores comes a sense of detachment from the physical envelope, which may be (and often is) considered to be a self-revelation of Dualism. This thing that was twisting itself about itself was a clearly subordinate Me, for I could order it to go faster, or to go slower, or to stop, or to go round the other way. My body was not Myself; and the feeling-realisation of this objective truth marked a point on the Way at which many searchers, as it seems to me, are content to rest prematurely.

At the end of two minutes I was a bored Dualist. But finally, a change occurred. As I persevered, a directing intelligence took charge of consciousness, and twisted me round without any apparent effort on my part; and this intelligence was indeed the Self, and indeed all kingdoms, principalities and powers. Glancing at my wrist-watch I was surprised to see that half an hour had passed.

I was in another current of Being, and a Dualist no longer/ Time, instead of standing still, raced by my body. Space, instead of dividing objects, linked them.

The distinction between creature and Creator melted away. The difficult idea of an individual soul communing with cosmos disappeared in the confident serenity of Unity. There was a merging and an Emergence; the self that writhed was but a reflexion of the true Self: its blood flowed in every vein, my soul was the world's: it was the face of the true sun of creation. A hymn echoed through my head, in time with my turning:

For ever with the Lord.
Amen; so let it be;
Life from the dead is in that word.

The lines took on an intenser meaning. Life from the dead: here in this body pent: home of my soul, how near at times Thy golden gates appear! . . .

Already, at Agra, I had had a glimpse of the ineffable. Great truths are simple. This one has been described in many ways, but best by Him who said: "Neither shall they say 'Lo here!' or, 'Lo there!'" . . .

Summer rode across the open lands of Anatolia. Women came out to bleed the poppy-beds that stretched red and white to the mountain of the horizon. Some were pretty, and some used to take the soldiers who formed our guard into the crops. We remained in prison.

In the autumn, Afion-Kara-hissar was visited by a

flight of storks who swooped and circled over us in their thousands, finally alighting near the black rock, where they formed black silhouettes against the sunset, with one leg tucked up, and backward-turning beaks. I used to dream of those storks, and of their enchanted journeys, and of Polly, an opium girl.

But chiefly I dreamed of freedom, and planned to regain it. That, indeed, was the bulwark of my sanity.

It would have been comparatively easy to have eluded our sentries, but Afion-Kara-hissar was separated from the coast by a belt of country where brigands and deserters roamed. Moreover, once the sea was reached, there were only a few places from which Greek islands could be reached, and those were closely guarded.

I discussed the matter with various friends—Robin Paul in particular—and we decided that our best and probably our only chance of escape was an indirect route. First we must reach Constantinople. The capital became in our minds a stepping-stone to freedom : we shammed sick : we tried to bribe a Greek doctor : we even inflicted wounds on various parts of our bodies. Robin had a bad ear, and I had displaced a bone in my nose by boxing, but it was not until I took to smoking opium with the Cypriote interpreter attached to the Turkish Commandant's office that my departure became possible. I will not say that I bribed him, but his intimacy helped me to bribe others.

Those nights I lay on a sofa with him, *couché à gauche*, as opium smokers say, weaving a tissue of deceit into the grey-white clouds encircling us, will always remain among the strangest memories of my life. The couches, the medley of cushions, the pipes, the profile of my host as he leaned over the green glimmer of the lamp which burned for the god to whom his heart was given, and the growth of that god in him, as pipe followed pipe ; and the beatitude in his eyes when they found the dream-world where the princes of the poppies reign, seem no more part of me now than a play, yet I did and felt and saw many unaccustomed things during that month of make-believe. And instead of reading philosophy or playing chess, I was engaged in a game whose stake was liberty.

Having reached Haider Pasha Hospital with the use of much gold as well as some guile, my purse was now empty. I needed two hundred Turkish pounds to be smuggled to Odessa, and I had only two lira.

However, there were other ways to freedom besides the sea-route, and when Robin and I were transferred to the Armenian Patriarchate at Psamattia (a suburb of Constantinople) an opportunity came to reach a friendly Christian house in the city.

The plan we made was simple. The window of the room in which we were imprisoned was set in an apparently sheer wall-face. Escape from it looked impossible, but as a matter of fact there were two small ledges of moulding under the window-sill, which would give us a foot-hold and a hand-hold, enabling us to gain the shelter of a near-by roof. From there we would work our way along other roofs to a place where we could drop down, out of the sight of sentries.

It was a good plan, because unexpected. To climb out of a window in view of six sentries seemed absurd, but we knew that sentries, like other people, rarely look up above their own height and rarely look for things that they do not expect.

So on the night appointed (and I must leave the reader to guess what agonies of preparation preceded it—the subterfuges by which we had procured maps of the city—the thrill of making ropes—the suspense of waiting—the schooling of accomplices—the intrigue with the Greek waiter who was to shelter us) we took off our boots, coiled five fathoms of linen-strip round our waists, stuffed our pockets and knapsacks with chocolates, a Baedeker, a compass, a pistol ; drank each other's healths in *raki*, and blew out our lamp as if going to bed. That was the signal to an accomplice, who had promised to engage the sentries opposite our house in conversation.

Crouched under the window-sill, we waited. The four sentries directly below us lolled on a bench, smoking and talking. Two more sentries were stationed fifty yards up the street. We heard the cheery voice of our comrade, offering cigarettes to our nearest guardians. That was our cue.

Robin went first and I followed an instant later.

The waiting had been anxious, but the moment my feet were on that blessed string course (how I blessed the architect who had designed it !) anxiety vanished and only the thrill of adventure remained. As we clambered along, like flies against the sheer wall, a passer-by in the street blew cigarette puffs almost into our nostrils. But no one looked up.

We gained the shelter of the parapet, surprised that our plan had succeeded, and devoutly thankful. Very cautiously, now that the worst was over, we wriggled on towards freedom. The parapet was lower than we thought, and the wriggling slow ; in order to take advantage of our cover we had to lie flat on our stomachs. After more than an hour of this progression, we had reached the place where we had thought to slip our rope, but found that just across the street an officer of the Fire Brigade sat at an open window, overlooking us. By the manner in which he peered about him it was evident that he was expecting someone to keep an appointment. He stared so intently that at one moment we thought he had seen us, as was very possible, for his window was on a level with our roof and only a few yards away.

Meanwhile the moon was creeping up the sky, and

about to flood us with such a radiance that even a love-sick officer of the Stamboul Fire Brigade could not fail to notice us. For a whole further precious hour this annoying Romeo kept watch, while we discussed him in whispers, and cursed feminine unpunctuality. At last, just as we had decided to let go the rope and take our chance (for our protecting belt of shadow had narrowed to inches) Romeo began to yawn, and stretch, and look towards his bed. He hesitated, yawned again, then gave up his hopes of Juliet and retired.

That was our moment.

We made the rope fast to a convenient ring in the parapet and stood up. Traffic had ceased in the street. The moon was at our backs and shone directly in the sentries' eyes. If they had seen us and fired we should at any rate have been uncertain targets.

I took a long breath and slid down, kicking the sign-board of a shop in my descent so that it clattered hideously. Robin, who followed, cut his hands to the sinews in his hurry.

In spite of the noise, no one stirred. A dog's yapping stabbed the silence.

Here we were, free, in an empty street. All the world was before us.

A moment before, the limelight of all the universe had seemed to shine on us ; and the noise we had made still echoed in my ears. Yet we had aroused not the smallest excitement in any breasts but our own.

Can you imagine the miracle, liberty-loving reader, that happens to a man who finds himself free after two-and-a-half years in Turkish prisons?

We were the proudest and happiest men in the world on that July night of Ramadan. The slothful years had vanished as we drew a breath. We lit cigarettes. We strolled away pretending we were Germans, and singing:

Lieb Vaterland, magst ruhig sein
Fest steht und treu die Wacht am Rhein.

Only once did we think we might be recaptured. As we were passing the Fatih Mosque, we heard a clatter on the cobbles behind us. A carriage was being galloped in our direction. We doubled into some ruins, and lay there. I trembled so much that I might have had a bout of fever. After all our success, the Psamattia garrison might still hunt us down.

The moon had reached her zenith: I looked up, and longed to be amongst the wispy clouds that crossed her light. A cat saw us, halted, watched us with glazing eyes. Then the carriage passed, empty of passengers, with a drunken driver. It rattled away into the night.

We emerged, and took our way through the streets of old Stamboul, under the chequered shade of vines, safe and free and triumphant.

CHAPTER XIV

CHRISTMAS, 1918

I cannot convey the thrill of that escape, for it will seem, as indeed it was, a fairly tame affair. Hundreds of prisoners have crept through the barbed wire of German camps, eluded bloodhounds, travelled long distances in disguise. But to me my first escape was from more than the Turks : I have freed myself also from an " inferiority complex."

We knocked softly at the door of the house in Sirkedji where we had arranged to hide ; then flattened ourselves in the shadow, ready for anything—welcome, betrayal, blackmail.

Nothing happened. We were about to knock again, when the door opened an inch, and I saw an eye, low down, level with my waist.

" May we come in ? "

" Are you the escaped prisoners ? " asked a child's voice, adding suspiciously, " we expected you two hours ago." (It was then four o'clock in the morning.)

" Better late than never," Robin said.

The door opened quickly, and we found a whole family of friendly people. Thémistoclé, the Greek waiter, and his mother, and aunt, and old grandfather, and the little twins who had greeted us.

We crept upstairs, careful not to awake the other inmates of the house, who were also fugitives from justice, according to Thémistoclé. When we paid him the fifty Turkish pounds we had promised him as the price of a week's shelter, his horn-rimmed glasses became dim with emotion.

" Everyone is starving here," he said thoughtfully. "Even the policemen go hungry for bribes. Yesterday one said to me, ' For the love of Allah find somebody for me to arrest.' "

" What did you answer ? " I asked.

" I said I would do my best. But of course I didn't mean it. Only one must be careful with the police."

" Yes, you must be very careful. And where are we to sleep ? "

We had been shown into an untidy room, with an icon shrine, and a rumpled bed.

" Here," said Thémistoclé—"my sister and I and the twins will turn out."

" Were you all—— ? "

" Oh, yes, rents are high, and we are poor people."

So we threw ourselves down, too exhausted to undress, and slept the sleep of free men.

Next moment, as it seemed to me, although in

reality three hours had elapsed, we were awakened by the twins, who looked on us as their especial charges, and taken down to the pantry for breakfast.

All that morning we stayed there, dozing by snatches, but always ready to bolt into the cistern if the police came. " The last escaped prisoner we had lived there by day," the twins told us. " He was a forger and has left his tools in the water."

By afternoon, we felt we were safe, and after sending the twins upstairs to see that the other lodgers were not about, we went up to our bedroom again, and discussed the situation.

There were various routes out of Constantinople. Robin Paul decided to try his luck by land, and after many intrigues, decided to board a Greek melon-boat bound for Rodosto. When he left me, he was disguised as an Arab beggar, and looked so villainous with his darkened face and hang-dog slouch that I feared he would be arrested at sight. But a touch of genius saved him : he carried a bowl of curds and half a cucumber, which gave him the aspect of a poor but honest man looking for a seat on which to eat his mid-day lunch.

My own plan was more comfortable, although no more successful than Robin's, as events proved. I was to leave Constantinople as the servant of a Russian Prince who was being repatriated to Tiflis, and make my way from there to Baghdad. Unfortunately the

Prince failed me, and Robin was caught at Malgara. He deserved better luck.

As for me, a good angel to escaping prisoners of war in the person of Miss Whittaker (now Lady Paul) took me under her wing and dressed me as a German governess in order that I might meet my Russian Prince without attracting the suspicion of the detectives who shadowed him. This plan was entirely successful as far as meeting him went, but Constantinople, where twenty thousand people were in hiding, and all were ready to sell their souls to escape, was an easier place to live in than to get out of. One night, Eveline Whittaker sent word to say that my Prince had been hustled off without having had time to say good-bye (or to return the money that I had lent him) and I had in consequence to make all my plans afresh.

There was now no object in dressing as a woman, and so I became a Hungarian mechanic, in a shabby bowler hat, and spectacles, and a dyed moustache. I began then to realise how easy it is to live unknown in a large city; and I had many opportunities of studying the "underworld," and of learning history as it is never written but most strangely lived by a people on the brink of disaster.

Things were on a hair-edge in Constantinople; a burst tyre made us think the revolution had come at last; we gossiped hopefully about the imminent downfall of Enver Pasha; and I attended a meeting of conspirators in the cellar of an hotel where we discussed how we might hasten the death-throes of the Committee of Union and Progress.

"We'll crucify the Turks," said a Greek— "and eat them in little bits." Then a bell rang, and the speaker, who was a waiter, hurried away to attend to his masters.

Rusty-looking muskets were unpacked. A silk flag was produced, stitched by Christian maidens, which was to fly from the summit of Aya Sofia when the Crescent was at last abased. Enthusiasm is contagious, and as the evening wore on I began to feel that I was helping to make history. Still more jubilant did I feel when my friends cashed cheques for me (written on half-sheets of notepaper) to the value of five hundred liras. My private promise to pay was worth more to them, apparently, than Turkish banknotes.

With plenty of money, I first bought myself a forged passport from Thémistoclé's friend (an imposing document, stamped, sealed, signed and delivered by the Governor of Constantinople; which certified, amongst other things that I was exempt from service in the Army owing to valvular disease of the heart) and then arranged with a certain Lazz that he should provide me with a motor boat to take me to Poti or Odessa.

This Lazz proved my undoing. We met at Thémistoclé's house and I was about to pay him one hundred pounds when the alarm was given and we found that detectives and police had broken in. I tried to bolt for the cistern, but the way was blocked. Presently Thémistoclé appeared with two policemen : his spectacles were broken ; he had a black eye and a bloody nose ; his collar had burst ; someone had rolled him in the dust. He trembled terribly as he protested that he had never seen me before, and no one believed him.

And so my five weeks' scheming ended in a sad little procession of two terrified children, a weeping woman, a miserable Greek, and some seedy-smart individuals wending their way to the Central Jail.

*** *** *** ***

How I was condemned first to an underground dungeon with criminals (the forged passport had been found in my pocket) and afterwards to solitary confinement ; how I stole a knife and fork from the prison restaurant and fused switches with them ; how I made friends with a nephew of the Sultan, a prisoner like myself, who had been sentenced to a month's detention for blowing out the brains of his tutor ; how this youth had a small black eunuch who used to bring me grapes and French novels ; how Robin and I escaped again ; and how, a fortnight before the Armistice was declared we stole General Liman von Sanders own motor car (a Mercèdes, which we hid in the back yard of the house we were occupying, and guarded with a performing bear) all sounds so improbable that I shall not write it down in detail.

I lay in bed in a house in the Cotswolds on the first Christmas Eve of peace, watching shadows from the fire passing over my brass hot-water jug. Outside, the waits were singing.

A few months ago, I was shivering on a couple of planks in a cellar littered with tomato skins and crusts of bread, with sleek rats and mangy men for my companions.

One of the prisoners had been shackled to the wall by chains rivetted to his wrists and ankles.

" One gets used to anything in time," he had told me, " except the bastinado. I have been here two years, accused of spying (they will never know the truth) and I am getting weak. But God is great. Unless they beat me again, I shall live for my vengeance."

They did beat him, however, and I saw it, when I was transferred to solitary confinement in an upper cell, whose window looked out on the place of punishment.

His ankles were strapped together to a pole, and the pole was raised on the shoulders of two men, so that he hung head downwards. A jailer hit the soles of his feet with a stick as thick as my wrist. He fainted, but the beating continued, for the sentence was fifty strokes. Had he survived, he would probably never have stood upright again, for the bones of his feet must have been crushed to pulp. They untied him and laid him flat on his back, and offered him water, but he made no sign, for he had died—of shock, I suppose, like my thoroughbred, The Devil.

There was one spy the less in Turkey.

How impossible that seemed to me now! Yet there were probably still men chained somewhere in that dungeon, and others being bastinadoed. I would search for no bugs to-night, and rise for no roll-call to-morrow. I had seen enough for a lifetime of wrath and bitterness and vermin. My pillow smelt of lavender.

CHAPTER XV

THE END OF SPORT AND SOLDIERING

For months I remained in London, ill. When at last I was allowed to return to my regiment, it was to take part in another war.

My hope had been that I should have some leisure to travel through India and learn more of her people and philosophies. Instead, I was jerked like a hooked fish from the waters of Yoga to the arid uplands of the North-West Frontier. My only consolation was that I was a Major now, commanding my own squadron.

In Waziristan I found that we had twice as many men under arms as Wellington had at Waterloo. We were paying £30,000 a year in subsidising the tribes to keep the peace (Naim Shah's section of the Afridis received £1,200 a year) and yet there was no peace. In fact, during the four years after the Great War, 578 civilians were killed, 669 were wounded, and 981 were kidnapped in 1,315 raids, and property to the value of £175,980 was looted between Quetta and Peshawar.

In Paris, statesmen talked of self-determination. Here men fought for it, and enjoyed the fighting very much, for instead of being compelled to descend into

British India for their booty it was now brought to their doors.

At Wana, the fort to which I was taking my squadron, the Mahsuds had recently looted four hundred rifles and about a million cartridges. Although the fort was now in our hands, they were still playing the devil in the surrounding country, sometimes carrying off fifty or sixty camels, sometimes sniping our camps, sometimes raiding isolated posts and looting £10,000 worth of ammunition. Our troops toiled through treacherous passes to make the world safe for democracy, while the Mahsuds praised Allah for our madness.

If the enemy were enjoying themselves, I was not, for my squadron had a difficult ride ahead of it through the mountains which led to Wana. From the bottom of my heart I cursed these contumacious highlanders, and the policy which sent vulnerable horses amongst them, instead of tanks and aeroplanes.

Where the river forks at Haidari Kach, I broke my fast with a young officer who was commanding the convoy of ammunition camels between that camp and the next, named Dargai Oba. He was full of enthusiasm, not yet having seen a year of service.

"I hope things'll jazz up just a little : it's dull seeing nothing but rocks," he said.

"Isn't the sniping enough?" I growled over my eggs and bacon.

We had had a mule hit during the night, who

had screamed until the humane killer had done its work.

"One gets used to anything. I've been out eight months and haven't yet seen one Mahsud in all this wilderness. I wish I was in Cavalry," he added, "it's slow work with camels, though the fishing isn't bad in the Tank Zam. If I catch any snow-trout, we'll have them for lunch at Dargai Oba."

Our advance guard galloped off, and I followed with the squadron, at a walk at first, then at a hound-jog. We obviously could not search every inch of country, so all that I attempted to do was to keep my weather eye lifting for cover, just as I used to look for landing grounds in Mesopotamia in case of engine failure.

We were in a pretty valley, whose charm was emphasised by the surrounding rockiness, and the peacock-hued sky above it, but its fields were untilled and its mulberry-shaded mill-streams idle, for the inhabitants were all busy with this profitable war. Wolf-eyes, I knew, were watching our movements, counting our rifles, observing how we marched. But along and above our route were small block-houses,—"Haig," and "Hunter," and "Ganpat" and "Goli," and so on to "Jess," and "Jill," and "Oba" and "Ox," each guarding a section of the road between the camps.

The Indian Officer who was riding beside me was called Valiant Tiger. The trumpeter's name was Happy Heart. The leading section was composed of Tiger Rose and Tiger Heart and Blooming Rose and Rose of the World: one hundred and twenty lives were in my hands, and many of us had baby Tigers and Roses and Kings. I hoped that the block-houses would do their work.

"Do you see those bushes," I asked my Merciful King "near the fat-tailed sheep?"

Naim Shah's eyes were better than my field-glasses.

"There is a boy with the sheep, Sahib."

"Of course. And behind him?"

I saw nothing, but asked on principle.

"You are right," said Naim Shah, standing in his stirrups and shading his eyes. "Away—away—aw-a-a-y on the skyline there is a woman moving."

"Head left wheel!"

I changed direction without checking, and signalled to the advance guard to do the same.

"I have seen it all," said Naim Shah. "There is a woman on the skyline. That is enough, Sahib."

"One?"

"One woman on the bare hill between the picquets. She is not grinding corn up there."

I called up the troop sergeant.

"Gallop back," I said, "and tell the Sahib with the convoy that there is a woman on that hill who may be carrying ammunition for men hidden in those bushes. Tell the Sahib we have taken a chukkar round, and that unless he hears any firing we shall be in Dargai Oba by the time he reaches this place. Gallop."

For an hour I trotted on, in a circle, returning to the road and dropping into a walk when close to camp, under the loopholes of "Jess" and "Jill."

We were about to enter the barbed wire of the perimeter camp, when half-a-dozen Lewis guns behind us began to chatter. Things had jazzed up, as my friend had hoped.

The squadron, however, could not fight amongst those boulders. Sending it on to water and feed, Naim Shah and I cantered back to see the battle.

Ten machine guns and a hundred men were pouring torrents of lead into the bushes, and into the rocks above them, but there was no answer from the enemy, who had already vanished.

A British corporal signaller had received a bullet through his throat. My friend was slightly wounded in the right hand.

One raider had had his skull smashed in. On the whole, the enemy's plans had miscarried.

A dozen Mahsuds had been hidden in those bushes. Opposite them, a party of knife-men had lain in wait, so close to our path that we must have almost ridden over them. They let us go, for their prey was less kittle cattle. The first volley from the riflemen killed the corporal. Then the knife-men rushed in.

"Ganpat" and "Goli" and "Greaves" had sprayed them with machine-gun fire. It was all over in thirty seconds, so my friend told me. A camel had escaped in the confusion, and it was presumed that the Mahsuds had it, with its four thousand rounds of ammunition. That worried my friend a great deal, and I could not console him by pointing out that he had done well not to lose more; and that he had caught a Mahsud instead of a snow-trout.

"Ganpat" continued firing, more to encourage itself than in any hope of finding an enemy amongst the echoing and empty rocks. For another month at least, no enemy would be seen in those parts.

The corporal we wrapped in a ground sheet, and he lies somewhere in that pleasant valley, where women are now grinding corn and their husbands making roads and driving cars.

In Wana, we did nothing whatever for several months.

The fortnight-old newspapers gave me news of politicians who complained of the heavy cost of the Indian Army. The Ali brothers preached of the wrongs of Turkey, and Mr. Gandhi declared that he would oppose the tribesmen of the North with soul force. . . . Apparently there was something in what the Mahatma said, for I was surprised and shocked to learn that some twenty *sillidar* cavalry regiments were to be abolished, my own amongst them. The authorities called the process " amalgamation," which sounded better than abolition, but came to the same thing, since our name, number and identity was to vanish.

Well, I thought, since my friends would soon be scattered, and I had long wanted to see horizons not discoverable from an Indian cantonment, I would " send in my papers " as soon as possible.

As if to confirm my decision, I met with a polo accident on my return from Waziristan.

It happened at Lucknow during a practice game. I was riding a big waler, fifteen hands and an inch without his shoes. I couldn't hold him, but the collision which ended my career as a cavalryman was not my fault. I was on the line of the ball. An opponent in front of me hesitated while trying to hit a backhander. I shouted to him not to stand on the ball. It was too late. My impression, as we collapsed together, was that I was being squeezed by some resistless power into his pony's brown quarters.

We sank down, and as I looked through the limbs of our entangled animals I observed that the other players were reining up and that the world seemed standing still. Instead of the whickering of whips, the rattle of hoofs, and the shouting, I had passed almost instantaneously into a state of silence and slow-motion.

I turned as I fell, drawing up my legs and tucking in my chin.

I was now being pressed down into the earth, without haste or apparent hope of escape. The other pony and its rider drew apart, but my waler stood on me. One of his hoofs was on the back of my neck, and the other on my right forearm. I carried him, with my forehead to the ground in an oriental *salaam*.

Which bone of me would break?

Time slipped backwards and forwards. With my brain I knew that my spine might crack, but with my imagination (working somewhere in the midriff) I saw myself getting up and dusting my breeches. Then every incident of my life connected with riding—from a frosty day in Ireland when my legs first gripped a horse to this uncomfortable conclusion—passed before me slowly. It was neat and logical. It was *karma*. Had I concussion of the brain?

No, for I was walking towards the refreshment table, arm in arm with two friends.

My arm was broken above the wrist.

"My head's all right," I said, "or isn't it?"

"Yes, of course, but you can't go on playing."

"Who said I could?"

"You did."

"How long ago was that?"

I could not remember how I had disentangled myself just a few moments before. All the way to hospital

I worried my friends for details of those mislaid seconds of my life, but I have never been able to trace them.

Yet what I have forgotten, as well as what remains vivid in memory, has its own tiny place in the Universe, and must therefore influence this book.

Nothing dies, not even the Present. Time is a tricky thing; and its sister, Space, preserves our voices and our gestures for all eternity. It is simply a matter of the point of view we take. Somewhere in space, I am still in that awkward position on the turf of a Lucknow polo-ground. Somewhere, also, the thunders of Trafalgar are echoing, and further back, the roars of a sabre-toothed tiger. But I wish I could always think as I did at that moment, and that I had not forgotten the images which then raced through my mind. . . .

CHAPTER XVI

THE FESTIVAL OF THE FISH-EYED GODDESS

While I lay in hospital, considering where I should go first after I had left the Service, a telegram came for me from the Army Department of the Government of India, suggesting that I should accompany an American author and his photographer on a tour through the country.

I accepted this offer immediately, for I could imagine no more delightful prospect. I tore up my resignation, sold my ponies, bought a typewriter, and as soon as my wrist was well enough I took the train to Delhi and began four crowded months of travel.

We went first to the plain of Panipat, my American friends and I, and then to the Ridge, overlooking the capital, from which one may contemplate the ruins of all the races that have held the sceptre of Hindustan.

Round us were six ruined Delhis, with their history of a thousand years of Empire, and the seventh Delhi was at our feet. We were on the roof of Hindu Rao's house, of Mutiny fame, which stands like a bridge upon a ship : a ship of rock, whose bow cuts into the dim sea of the plains.

" There is more land in this country than in Europe from Norway to Sicily," I said, " and more languages, religions, gods, people. If you took the peasants of it only, and stood them shoulder to shoulder, like an army, they would girdle the earth five times at the Equator. I knowit is a weariness to tell you such things, but I can't help it, for you travellers always forget the peasants."

" Don't they want to rule their own country for themselves, like the lawyers and merchants and politicians ? "

" I don't know," I answered. " It is certain they want a just king and light taxes, but whether they want democracy is doubtful. I don't think any Englishman knows. We are colonisers and traders, not wet-nurses. We are only a drop in the ocean of this humanity. A couple of thousand individuals cannot maintain themselves in a population three times the size of the United States without the tacit consent of those governed. If united India wants us to go, we shall vanish as the mists will vanish from the plain of Panipat at dawn to-morrow. But if we did, our tradition would remain, for India never forgets . . ."

At that, the jackals began howling, and we returned to our hotel for dinner.

***   ***   ***   ***

The next day we motored to Nizam-ud-din's tomb, where Jehanara lies, the lovely princess whose modest epitaph was composed by herself in the age which saw the glories of the Taj : " Let nothing but green conceal me. Grass is the best covering for the poor, the humble, the transitory Jehanara, disciple of the holy men of Chist, and daughter of the Emperor Shah Jehan."

Into her history is woven, by the twists and quirks of fate, our own Imperial destinies. But for her, British India would have had a different birth.

The story begins by Jehanara's maid upsetting an oil-lamp in the palace of Shah Jehan. Jehanara tried to save her, and in doing so she scorched herself about the face and hands. Shah Jehan was in a fever of anxiety about his daughter : the æsthete as well as the parent in him demanded that the best physician in his Empire must attend its loveliest princess.

Thus it happened that Gabriel Boughton, the surgeon of the English factory at Surat, arrived at Agra. Although hampered by the etiquette of *purdah* (he was only allowed to feel his patient's pulse from behind a curtain) he not only cured Jehanara but saved her beauty flawless. As reward, he would take nothing for himself, but asked that a charter should be given to the East India Company to trade in Bengal.

These are the threads of *karma* that go to the making of ant-heaps and Empires : a clumsy slave-girl, a kind princess, and an altruistic doctor who asked for the charter on which the British built Calcutta. All round Delhi one may see the warp and woof of modern India.

At Tughlakabad, for instance, whither we went on leaving the grave of Jehanara, we found the hereditary well-jumpers of the Moghul court still plying their profession. In 1922 some twenty of these men were alive, and all still active, including the eldest, who was ninety-nine.

The shaft was eighty feet deep and only eight feet wide, so that if the jumpers had taken off with the slightest outward impetus they would have hit the sides and killed themselves. The only way to reach the bottom in safety was to step off as if going down a stair, and this the old men did.

One after another they went down, making a noise like popping corks. It was not very exciting, but it was extremely whimsical. Obviously the Great Moghuls had enjoyed the sport, for they had cut away one side of the well in a ramp to the water-level, and had made five archways in the shaft, so that they could sit with their princesses to watch the jumpers flash by.

The old men insisted on going through their performance once again, for they enjoyed the risk, and our admiration, irrespective of the reward I had offered them. With glistening eyes, naked, proud, they came to me in turn after their jump, and extended trembling hands.

"This is the India of tradition," I could not help observing, "the real India, rooted in the past. All round us history is being kept alive by people instead of books. Near here there is a lime tree, under which Akbar's favourite musician, Tansen, was buried four centuries ago, about the time when this well-jumping began. To this day, the strolling players of India pluck leaves from it, and eat them, that their voices may have the sweetness of 'that honey-tongued parrot without an equal.' Tansen's memory survives; and the tradition of the Taj survives in the craftsmen who are working at their hereditary trades here and at Agra; and John Nicholson, who took Delhi, is still worshipped by a sect in the Punjaub. Even Alexander the Great is remembered, for there is a legend that at a spot where he rested in the jungle the tigers come out on nights of the full moon, to sweep the place clean with their tails."

While I discoursed the eldest well-jumper came up to us, wringing his wet, white beard.

"Sahib, what are we to do with our boys?" he asked. "Government has forbidden us to teach them to jump, saying it is dangerous, and that they must be educated. Are they to sit in schools with idol-worshippers instead of learning our ancient craft?"

"Who is to know what you teach them?"

"That is true," he chuckled, "and on bright nights we do still show them how the trick is done, beginning from the bottom archway. But their heads are so full of this new tyranny of education that I doubt whether they will ever have our skill."

"May Allah, Who is a reader of hearts, keep your descendants in the right path!"

"Ay, Sahib, He knows best. But a living is hard to earn. Before the Mutiny a rupee bought twenty pounds of flour, instead of half-a-pound, as to-day. If our descendants are to become *babus* instead of well-jumpers, who is to support us?"

Alas, I did not know. I gave the old man my blessing and a small extra gift.

We went northwards now, travelling three days and nights to Naim Shah's village across the border, where we enjoyed an illicit tea-party (for British officers are forbidden to cross the frontier that divides India from Afghanistan) and an Arabian night's entertainment of Afridi raids, vendettas, and other adventures, some of which I had to modify very severely in translation. We visited Bannu, where my youth was passed, and Jandola, with its memories of snipers, and Dera Ismail Khan, and Quetta; and from there, with one of those sudden transitions which are always possible in India, we journeyed south to the rock-hewn temples of Ajanta, where the painters and craftsmen of a thousand years ago have left their portrayal of a civilisation that rivals that of the High Renaissance in Italy.

The contrast was complete between the living frontier and this world of stone. Instead of shepherds with their fat-tailed sheep here was a lovely little Queen of Benares fainting in the lap of her negro slave ; instead of dancing boys and camels and well-kept rifles and daggers, the kings of the frescoes were worshipping their golden geese, and blue gods were embracing fawn-eyes *shaktis* in mysterious attitudes and ecstasies.

Who can say why nations rise and fall, why the spirit of genius alights here and not there ? Everywhere in India this puzzle is seen of civilisations that triumphed for their hour, and have now gone down to dust and white ants. Consummate skill and tireless patience were lavished on Ajanta. The chisels of a million workmen hammered on those cornices ; the desires of a race for beauty, for romance, for true religion are embodied here in stone and paint. But over the work of the painters and sculptors stands the doom of time. The darkness of Ajanta is full of death.

On the plinth of one of Buddha's altars, polished by the foreheads of an unknown multitude of worshippers, I saw a dead bat lying, with a snarl on its rat-face ; and I noticed then that there were bats everwhere, flying among the pictures, hanging from the pillars.

Outside, the sun beat down upon a barren valley.

*** *** *** ***

The pageant of India that passed before us confirmed this sense of the futility of human endeavour. The Residency at Lucknow, with its flag still flying; Amritsar with its field of slaughter; the *sati* memorials of Muttra; Bijapur with its whispering gallery, and its gold-and-ivory gun which used to be manned by artillery-men in pink fleshings; Podanur where the recalcitrant Moplahs were suffocated by a ghastly mistake; French Pondicherry where Dupleix dreamed of Empire; Cochin where the Jews of the tribe of Manasseh (exiled from Palestine after the destruction of the Second Temple) are now dying of elephantiasis; Mrs. Besant at Adyar, undaunted at the age of seventy-five, busy with her Messiah and telling us in her vibrant voice that "the coming of His hour is nigh, when He shall come again to mankind, as He did so often in the past"; and more than all, Cape Cormorin, the southernmost point of India, which has seen Roman and Phœnician galleys pass, and missionaries, merchants, pirates, politicians, each with his own doomed dream of conquest—all these places and people seemed to us but shadows that have passed across the peace of India.

We dipped down the Braganza Valley into Portuguese Goa and strolled through the cloisters of the Cathedral of Bom Jesus, where St. Francis Xavier lies under a magnificent altar. Round us were the ruins of Goa Dourada, the richest city in India in the sixteenth century, now a village of a few huts.

Through a broken gateway, which bore the deer-crest of Vasco da Gama, I could see the Blue Mountains under the gathering monsoon. A storm was about to break : a bell tolled : it seemed to ring for an *auto da fé*. Thinking myself back across the centuries, I saw the Cathedral Square filling with priests and people. The bell rang slowly now, as if for souls about to pass : there was a sharpness in the air. . . . I rubbed my eyes : wood smoke drifted across the courtyard : a lizard watched me from a crumbled wall. The Holy Inquisition was done with and forgotten, like Golden Goa, like every alien effort at domination over the apparently-defenceless millions who live between the breakers of Cape Cormorin and the snows of Tibet.

And now to Madura, where the Festival of the Fish-eyed Goddess is in progress.

Minakshi was a princess in Madura long ago ; a girl with long and lustrous eyes, who subdued all earthly princes and even the heavenly deities with her beauty. She had three breasts, but when she met Siva her third breast disappeared, and she knew then that she stood in the presence of her Lord.

The marriage was arranged and an enormous concourse of people assembled—as to-day—in the river-bed of the Vaigai. Amongst the chief guests was Minakshi's brother, Alagar ; but by some unfortunate slip the date of the wedding was wrongly given in his invitation, so that he arrived late, and found that the ceremony had already been performed.

He went away in anger, and rested on the far side of the river. Every year since then, he comes late to the feast, retires, sulks. . . . All over Southern India this story is told, and it brings together a hundred and fifty thousand people, very gentle and simple and scantily-clothed, to celebrate the anniversary of Fish-eyed Goddess's marriage, and her brother's disappointment.

From the bridge spanning the Vaigai, we look down on a moving, mixing mass of colour : dark blue elephants, light blue water, yellow sand, green trees, gold chariots, pavonine tinsels of fans and shawls, under a turquoise sky which stuns the eyes with its hard brightness. I have seen crowds as big, but never a kaleidoscope like this.

The heat is murderous, for the monsoon which has been threatening us for a week has not yet broken. Young girls glisten under their load of anklets and bracelets. Soon their eyes will lose their lustre, and their skin its glow of bronze, but to-day in their prime, with the kiss of so much sun upon them, they are as lovely as Minakshi herself. Their elders fan themselves, wilting. Terra-cotta babies droop on their mothers' shoulders. Alagar himself feels faint in his marquee, and frankincense is burned under his nostrils to revive him.

Now there is a booming of mortars. Priests with forked white eyebrows are clearing a way for the enamelled steeds of the goddess. There is a crowding and a crying and a scampering of sacred cows.

When she arrives, the voice of the multitude is hushed: elephants raise respectful trunks: men, women and children touch finger-tips together and bow themselves down in a silence that is frightening after so much clamour.

The heart of India seems to miss a throb ; the people are sorry for the belated wedding guest, sulking in his tent, across river.

But then their mood changes and gives place to gaiety and clamour. Swings and merry-go-rounds and hawkers and religious freaks compete for coppers ; there is a brisk business in mangoes and fans ; a goat is being sprinkled with water before its head is chopped off ; pilgrims are having their heads shaved ; a priest adorns another with the crimson *tika* of his caste ; children are playing thoughtful games in the sand, like a motionless hop-scotch ; and their mothers are comparing their new bangles. But for this heat, I could stay here for hours, watching India at play and prayer.

Yet what could I learn of the people's heart, so far from mine ? If I were six years old I might understand it better, but now . . . I float back towards the great temple of Madura upon a stream of pilgrims.

Suddenly that strange, orgiastic pile hulks above me,

tier upon tier of sculptured reliefs that are by turns monstrous and graceful and lewd. This is only one corner of it : it is repeated in the east and west and north, and it is one of a thousand such temples. What an extraordinary people it was who made these gods and goddesses and hermaphrodites of stone, that go swarming up to the sky in exuberant confusion, in renunciations and exaltations inconceivable, and cruelties and tendernesses I cannot begin to fathom ! If I could know who built this terrible place (but no one knows) or what these pullulating deities are about, or even why Minakshi had three breasts, I might begin to understand this India of the South.

Across the open courtyard, men and women are surging in a maze of corridors. Hidden in the darkness of the central shrine stands a little *lingam*. The courts and shrines and great carved pyramids which surround it have been built on an esoteric design which only the priests understand, and they but dimly.

Somewhere in the temple a parroquet is screaming as if Satan were pulling his tail-feathers, but where or why I cannot tell, for I may not set foot beyond the threshold.

Indeed, I do not want to, for I am afraid.

CHAPTER XVII

JAGANATH, LORD OF THE WORLD

At Puri, near Calcutta, where Jaganath rides in his car, we found that the festival of the year was not due for a few days yet, so we decided to bathe and then to seek out a temple official to inform us about Jaganath, and his brother Balarama and his sister Subhadra, those wooden idols that have been the adored of millions for uncounted centuries.

Fortunately—for the priests were not very informative—I had an introduction to the Superintendent of the shrine, and found him ready to talk.

We broached first a delicate subject—the sculptures of the Black Pagoda at Konarak. How, we asked, could any community that claimed the respect of the modern world condone representations of depravity such as those which we had seen at Konarak a few days before (even admitting that they were mingled with other figures of singular beauty and grace)?

"You must remember," said the Superindentent, "that these sculptures are old. We Hindus need not justify the manners of a franker age. But we *can* justify them, if you like, by comparing the teaching of ancient Konarak with that of modern Vienna. We had a school, as you have a school, that maintains that the roots of psychology lie in sex. You in the West are inclined to begin the consideration of psychology with your brain, instead of with your nerves. Yet the nerves made the brain. You must learn to control feeling before you can control thought, if you would not be meshed in illusion."

"That is the lesson of Konarak?"

"Yes, in so far as the artists who worked there were concerned with anything but beauty. They idealised Woman, without whom we could not be born, nor enjoy," he said. "To know Woman, through the ministering senses and the attendant angels is the greater wisdom. Humanity has been shaped by Her and through Her it must be saved. The *lingam-yoni* is the symbol of the entry of spirit into matter, without which the world could not have been made, and through whose right function it must be sustained. Our human *lingam-yoni* is but a tiny fraction of the cosmic energy, a spawning between a certain range of heat and moisture, beyond which extend Himalayan heights and unutterable abysses; but even what we have is the greatest of mysteries humanity may contemplate. It is the link between the visible and invisible, the conductor of souls, the fountain of religion. If even physical love (to say nothing of the other kind) ceased on earth then the love of God would disappear, for its knowers would not exist."

"There is a Yoga relating to your worship?"

"Certainly, the *Laya-siddhi*, by which we know the subtlest of the subtle, who holds within Herself the mystery of creation. Even in the West, you have such a philosophy, but disguised, for your whole material prosperity is based on sex-control, which drives you out to conquer new worlds, partly in compensation for what has been denied and partly to enable you to gain the object of your desire. Up to a point our teaching is the same, but ours is not inculcated through repression. Modesty and continence are virtues necessary to every kind of Yoga, in the East as in the West, but that does not mean the thwarting of natural functions."

"Not thwarting, but control," I agreed. "Yes, in the West we are becoming choked with desires—and not only for sex—which are driven into the Unconscious because they cannot find their normal expression."

"You are playing with fire, it seems to me. Many of your amusements and most of your ambitions are unnatural. So are your hours of work, your hours of sleep, your late marriages, your cheap reading, your patent foods. You cannot live unnaturally and have natural sex lives; and unless you do have natural sex lives either your civilisation will perish, or your women will revolt."

" Our women are patient, *pandit-ji*, as yours were under conditions that condemned them to burn themselves alive when their husbands died."

" Yours have no husbands, and burn out their souls in a loneliness more cruel than the fire of the *sati* sacrifice."

" I wonder if they would think so ? "

" Perhaps not. The agonies of the Unconscious are not always known, even to the sufferer. But there is a vast secret misery in all the cities of Europe and America, chiefly among your women, but also among men who have been sacrificed to your chaste commercial Mammon. Living as you do, you have neither the time nor the energy for love. Your women are not as happy as ours. They have a fuller exterior life, but a starved interior life. Under our caste system, with all its faults, the deep unseen existence of humanity is better provided for."

" Admitting that for the sake of argument," I said, " I still do not see how the portrayal of depravity is going to help humanity. Even here in your temple I am told there are frescoes in the corridors——"

" —As ugly as a treatise on psycho-analysis ! " exclaimed the Superintendent. " Certainly they are shocking, for they are meant to shock. Everything connected with the worship of Jaganath is symbolical, and its meaning lies deep in the truths of our religion. The people understand what they can of such things :

we do not demand the impossible. Surely it is the same everywhere? The worshipper can receive only what his brain or his feeling-realisation can sustain. Many things must remain hidden. The approach to the shrine of Jaganath, for instance, is by avenues corresponding to man's life in the exterior and interior worlds. First there are the snares of the senses, portrayed by paintings and sculptures which your missionaries describe as of 'appalling indecency.' Is Freud indecent? Can truth be indecent? I am sure that future ages will look on our Tantrik psychology of the Unconscious with understanding. Until a man is master of his gross body, he cannot see the Godhead.

"But remember," he continued, "that we are only at the exterior threshold of the divinity symbolised by an earless, legless block of wood about a yard high, which is Jaganath. If the worshipper be blinded by his carnal appetites in these outer courts, he must return and compose his mind, for he is not worthy of the god. Only with undistracted senses may he enter the Dancing Hall, where the *deva-dasis* portray the rhythms of creation, not any longer in stone or paint, but in their living bodies. That is the second stage. From there, the worshipper passes to the Audience Chamber, where his eyes grow gradually accustomed to the Light Invisible. I wish I could escort you round the temple, Sahibs, and explain these things personally. We are not fanatical in Puri, but unfortunately such libels about our worship were published some years ago that now no European may enter the Lion Gate."

"We never expected to see the inside of the temple, *pandit-ji*," I said, "and although I am a Christian—or because of it—I detest the methods of some of our earlier missionaries. But now all that is changed, I hope."

"Yes, you have come to understand that you need not attack our religion in order to uphold yours. The Hindus are the most catholic-minded race the world has ever seen. We have never persecuted any faith. We have never proselytised any people. All we ask is to be left alone."

"But frankly, you will admit, I suppose, that all human ordinances have their defects, even those of *Manu*? Surely there must be reform in such matters as *purdah*, child-marriage, and the position of widows?"

"The women of India will change their customs sooner than you think, Sahib. But they will not change their religion, for our sacred books have seen very far into their hearts."

"Yet they teach such things as that a woman should worship her husband's big toe in the morning: isn't that a relic of slavery?"

"No. A thousand times no! Woman with us is a queen, not a slave. She is not man's inferior, but a part of him. The most important part, perhaps. Without her, he is nothing. If she smears his foot with sandal-wood paste at dawn, that may seem strange to you, but to us it is an act of reverence to the Creator who has the two sexes in Himself. It is done for the glory of *Hara*, who is half-man and half-woman, and whose adored spouse is part of her own being. Your new psychology teaches the same thing in other words when it asserts that the unconscious part of the individual is oppositely sexed. And I beg you not to credit the stories you hear about Hindu women being frail and fainting creatures. Have you heard two washerwomen talking to each other across a river ? The Hindu wife is mistress in her own house. She is worshipped as the mother of the race, as the keeper of tradition, as the partner in religious rites, as giver of life, and creative goddess in human form. Marriage is the pivot of our religion. The union of the sexes is not a concession to the flesh with us, but a sacrament. On the bridal night the husband must enter his wife's room mediating on *Praja-pati*. He must touch her and say : 'HRING, O bed ! Be thou propitious to the begetting of a good offspring between us two.' He must sit with his face east or north, and looking at her and embracing her with his left arm, he must touch her head one hundred times, saying KLING, and touch her chin one hundred times, saying AING, and touch her throat twenty times, saying SHRING, and again SHRING one hundred times over each of her breasts. And so on. There is also a ritual for conception, weaning, the end of childhood, the beginning of adolescence, marriage, home-making, and dissolution —all the chief moments in the life of the spirit from the time when it enters the womb, to the time when it rises from the burning pyre. From birth to death, and dawn to dark, Jaganath is saviour of our people."

"You have said that he is only a block of wood, *pandit-ji*. How can he also be a vital force in your lives? To us it seems hard to understand how he and his relations can be more than dressed-up dolls."

"It is our age-long veneration that has brought them to life. Ours is a religion of the Unseen, but it must have a focus."

"A bright object on which the mind of the multitude may concentrate?"

"Not quite. Jaganath is what you call a catalyst," said the Superintendent, "a mysterious agent that out of two things induces a third. Out of our religion and our people, he has made the Car Festival. A hundred and twenty *deva-dasis* dance in his honour; he has twenty temple elephants, a wardrobe such as no king of the earth possesses, and two cellars, knee-deep in pearls and rubies and other votive jewels, which have not been opened for three centuries. He has three thousand panders who travel throughout the country on his behalf, arranging for parties of pilgrims to pay their homage to the Lord of the World; and a thousand regular priests. I cannot tell you of all the wealth and worship he has received since the beginning of time. He is an image, but he is also a god, since we have desired him."

"That is a miracle," I said.

"You mean, Sahib, that you think that the age of miracles has passed? Not so. We still believe in them."

"Can you tell us, then," I asked, in order to change the subject, "whether there are any Yogis now living in Puri who possess those supernatural powers of which we hear in the West?"

"The rope trick and the mango trick? I have heard of such things," said the Superintendent. "But I have never seen any of them. If they happen, they are not supernatural, but due to collective suggestion. Let me advise you to beware of miracles made to order, especially in this country. In India a real student of Nature's finer forces never wants for a living, and never produces phenomena for cash. If you are interested in experiments of an unusual kind, however, there is a Yogi here who is carrying out researches in animal *Kundalini*. He is said to be able to resurrect dead sparrows."

"Could we visit him?" I asked.

"Of course. Go to his bungalow by the sea. Anyone can tell you where he is. His name is Babu Bisudhanan Dhan."

"Could you give us an introduction?"

"That is quite unnecessary, but you had better tell him I sent you. . . . He is being watched by the police."

he added with a laugh. " In Europe of the Middle Ages he would have been burned as a sorcerer ; here on the contrary he is honoured as a teacher. His friends have equipped a laboratory for him in Calcutta, and have given him a house in Benares, and a bungalow here so that he can carry on his work wherever the fancy takes him. You will find a group of his students with him, if you go in the morning."

" I remember that I was told of the *babu* years ago," I said, " when I was a youngster in Bareilly. Certainly we shall call on him, *pandit-ji*. Couldn't we go this afternoon ? "

" In the afternoon he may be invisible."

" Doesn't he receive callers then ? "

" Well, he sometimes vanishes."

" Vanishes ? "

" Floats away."

Here was something that my American friends had not been expecting to find—a man who could raise the dead and vanish !

Accompanied by Naim Shah, who carried the Americans' cameras, we descended on the *babu* next morning and found him teaching his disciples in the verandah of his house, just as the Superintendent had said.

He was a very fat man, wearing nothing but the usual loin-cloth and the Brahminical thread. He sat in a long chair with his legs curled under him, talking to ten or a dozen white-habited, middle-aged Bengalis, most of whom wore spectacles. Seeing us, he nodded casually, finished what he was saying, and then smiled.

The Superintendent may, of course, have warned him of our possible arrival, but if so, he had not told his pupils, who demanded explanations of our visit from Naim Shah, and demanded them rather nervously, I thought. The *babu* himself remained inscrutable. Naim Shah looked sheepish ; he disliked being mixed up with such matters and left me to explain.

" I heard of the Mahatma's fame many years ago," I said, " and I have ventured to bring my friends here so that they may meet a great Yogi before they return to the United States."

" What is it," a disciple asked me, in English, " that you want the Mahatma to do ? "

" Anything he pleases," I answered. " We want to learn something of his supernatural powers, if that is at all possible ; and at any rate to enjoy the privilege of talking to him."

A few words of Bengali passed between the pupil and his master, then the former answered :

" The Mahatma is in the middle of a lecture about the aspects and appearances of our Lord the Sun, whose energies he can control. If you like, he can summon any scent to appear before us out of the circumambient ether."

I glanced quickly at the nude *babu* to see if he were joking. His eyes were exceptionally large : they blinked rapidly in my direction, as if I were some new but not unpleasant kind of creature.

"We should be honoured if the Mahatma would do this," I said solemnly.

"May we take his picture first," my friend suggested, "now that the light is good ?"

I translated.

The Mahatma had no objection. He posed readily, and with a dignity that few of us clothes-cramped people possess.

"He lives on a banana a day," the English-speaking pupil told us, with a kind of paternal pride, "and such is his power over etheric vibrations that he can quicken his molecular activity until he floats in the air. We have seen this, both here and in Benares. No one knows his age. He says he is fifty, but we think he is nearer three hundred years old. During my lifetime he has been thirty years in Tibet, studying the radiations from the sun and moon. Before that he was travelling for seven years in the jungles of Central India, where wild beasts followed him like dogs."

"A banana a day !" repeated my friend, looking at the Mahatma's solid form.

"And a little water," our informant added, "that is

all. He makes these concessions to mortality in order to remain on the earth plane. He never sleeps. His power over Nature is simply a question of using the rays from our Lord the Sun."

"What about the sparrows?" my friend asked.

"Unfortunately we have no sparrows here, or the Mahatma would show you. He brings life to them after they are dead by using the sun's rays in a certain way. The sparrows are strangled by a sweeper, and left in the sun for four hours, to make sure that they are dead. The Mahatma then lets a little light fall on them through a magnifying-glass, using a *mantra* taught to him by his Tibetan *guru*, whose vibrations can reach the heart of birds. Their feathers begin to ruffle. They move their wings and open their beaks. In a moment they are on their feet, hop about, flutter away. It is very curious."

"Most remarkable," we agreed.

Meanwhile the Mahatma had curled himself up again in his chair. He called for cotton-wool and a magnifying-glass, which were brought to him by a disciple. I watched this man carefully without being able to detect the slightest sign of collusion. Indeed, on making enquiries about him afterwards, I learned that he was a respectable small banker: this fact would not indeed preclude his being a conjuror's accomplice, but makes it less probable.

The Mahatma took the cotton-wool in his left hand

and the glass in his right, focusing a spot of light upon the wool. Immediately the room was impregnated with the perfume of attar of roses.

He waved the scent away with his hand, and I certainly had the impression that it vanished at his gesture.

" What other scent would you like to come ? " he asked me in Hindustani, with a smile that showed two rows of perfect white teeth.

I suggested violets, and instantly the room was full of the scent of violets. Then I suggested eau-de-Cologne, and there was a hitch, for he did not understand.

" Name any Indian scents, and he will bring them at once," said the pupil.

My friend suggested carnations, but I could not remember the Urdu for them, and the pupil could not visualise them from my description.

" Can he make the scent I am thinking of appear ? " I asked, " even though I cannot give it a name ? "

The Mahatma smiled and shook his head.

So I named musk, and sandalwood, and opium, and heliotrope, and flowering bamboo, and nicotine plants at evening. Each came instantly. There was nothing near him that could have served as a receptacle. He had no sleeve, no table, nothing but a magnifying-glass and a piece of cotton-wool.

" Has the Mahatma powers of hypnotism as well as the power to direct solar energy ? "

I asked the question to the room at large. There was a general laugh.

" In one instant, the Mahatma could hypnotise all of us together," said a little man in horn spectacles, who looked like a shop-keeper, " or all of us separately," he added.

" May we photograph him while he is summoning a scent? " my friend asked.

The Mahatma seemed to be getting bored, but consented to be snapshoted twice, while he produced out of the air—or was it out of our imaginations ?—the heavy odour of jasmine and the acridity of burning cattle-dung. The latter seemed to make my eyes water, and if that was imagination then everything is of the stuff of dreams.

We three men of the West had all had some training in the use of our eyes, yet we were led by our noses into an impasse on this hot, bright June morning.

Acknowledge a miracle I would and will not. With my brain I refused and rejected it, but with my body I was fain to believe. And now another emotion over-rode curiosity. I wanted to escape the contagion of credulity that the Mahatma had induced in us.

My friend suggested that in a few days' time the Mahatma might show us the resurrection of sparrows. He smiled and stared ahead of him, vaguely, until I repeated the observation. Then he spoke in Bengali, instead of Urdu ; and not to me, but to a pupil.

" He says that he is not fond of crowds and will not be here for the Car Festival," said the interpreter.

" Ask him if he knows why we came ? " my friend persisted.

Again the answer had to be translated from Bengali.

" He says he knows, but that his *guru* told him long ago that such questions should never be answered."

Silence.

I was conscious of something hostile in the atmosphere.

" I fear we have been interrupting the Mahatma's lecture," I said, and paused, in case he should deny it. As he did not, I observed that we were grateful to him for the time he had given us, and that if it was convenient we would now take our leave.

" You are masters in this house," said the Mahatma, bowing in his deck-chair. " You have greatly honoured me."

" On the contrary, it is we who have been honoured."

What had we seen ? Conjuring ? Black magic ?

" The *babu* may be a fraud or a hypnotist," I suggested, " or he may have some way of harnessing etheric vibrations. Anyway, he has a band of disciples who believe in him sufficiently to pay for his work. Experiments like this have been continuing for centuries, along lines very different from those of any Western science. Perhaps there is something stirring, something shaping itself out of the mists of superstition on this old continent which will spread its influence over all the world. Even along our own narrow lines, Indians have arisen whose extraordinary attainments are unquestionable. Disbelieve in this *babu* if you like, but you must accept Bose, Raman, Meghnad Saha, Tagore, Gandhi. By whatever standard you judge them they are men of distinction, and there will be many more, when we discover more of India."

And the more I considered these matters in which my mind disputed with my senses, the less confident I became that my brain was right.

The monsoon had broken, but pilgrims were still flocking into the wet and insect-ridden city. A hundred thousand of them had arrived, and billions of insects of every kind.

At dinner these latter made a massed attack upon our lamp and fell in battalions around it : their scouts even reached our soup. Our mosquito-curtains were coated with praying mantis and beetles, moths, winged ants.

Outside the hotel, pilgrim waggons creaked by. Ox-nose to tailboard of the cart ahead, a multitude of creatures were being drawn into the flame of the Lord of the Age of Iron.

*** *** *** ***

It is early morning. From the Lion Gate, for a mile of broad avenue leading to the Garden Temple, the concourse of the people of Jaganath makes one vast composite body of brown skin and white cloth.

We are in a roped-off enclosure, containing high officials and the vehicles of the gods. The cars are cottages on wheels, with thirty-foot towers, betinselled and beflagged, and embroidered with celestial beasts. That of Jaganath is a little bigger than the others, and has sixteen wheels : the others twelve. They are made new each year, being broken up after the return from the Garden Temple, in order that the sacred wood may be sold to the people.

In front of the cars sit the drivers of the gods, magnificent wooden coachmen in a striped livery of yellow. They are quaint figures on the ground, whipless, reinless, grinning at the crowd, with their elbows out in regular coaching style ; but when the gods take their seats they will be demigods themselves, driving three thousand pilgrims each. The ropes to which the worshippers will be harnessed lie coiled beside them.

In this enormous crowd, there is not the colour and animation of the Madura festival, for the people are squatting ; but the bourdon note of all these blended voices drowns the roar of the sea a few hundred yards away. Priests move among the people with fans, and sprinkle them with holy water. There is a coming and going at the Lion Gate. We are packed to suffocation, and blanketed under clouds. The air is electric in every sense, for the monsoon overshadows our bodies and the gods our souls.

It is now eight o'clock and I hear that the gods are not likely to hurry over their toilette. The morning hymn must be sung to them, camphor burned before their beds, their libations poured, the holy food offered, and their teeth cleaned by rubbing their reflection in a sheet of burnished gold. These things will take time, and I shall breakfast while the gods make ready.

Ten o'clock. Two policemen are with us, but even with their help it would be impossible to return to the Temple Square, so packed is it. Instead, we enter the back of a house which has a balcony overlooking the car enclosure. Amongst the elect, I see the temple Superintendent rushing about with a garland of marigolds round his neck. He is signalling to a mounted Englishman in khaki—the District Superintendent of Police.

Subhadra is coming. Ripples of excitement spread

over the surface of the brown and white mass, as if it were stretching its muscles in the sunshine. The panders tell the pilgrims that the sister of the Lord of the World is coming : the pilgrims lift up their voices : the panders join hands in worship : the pilgrims join theirs : the panders sprinkle and fan the multitude, and its voice becomes the purr of one tremendous tiger.

An hour passes, and Balarama arrives like Subhadra to take his seat. Here and there a fainting woman is carried away. The crowd talks without pause.

It is not until high noon that the climax comes, when a shimmer of white plumes and a waving of wild, braceleted arms heralds the entry of the Lord of the World through the Lion Gate. Now nothing can restrain the crowd : the tiger rises, roars, lashes its tail, sweeps away the roped-off enclosure and ramps over the cars.

In this welter it is hard to see Jaganath himself, but I catch a glimpse of a painted mouth, a hooked nose, jewels. A hundred backward-moving priests precede him : a hundred bear his litter : a thousand come behind. For this occasion he has been provided with gold hands and feet. He has trumpeters and peacock fans and a Noble Guard, like the Pope in Rome. A Rajah, with jewelled broom, sweeps the ground before him. With each step of the bearers, Jaganath's shading fan comes forward, as if keeping time to the cries of his people. The sun emerges to join in the rejoicing.

Jaganath is ready to begin his drive.

The British policeman takes his place in front of the car. Jaganath cannot be disregarded by the temporal power, for men and women still sometimes throw themselves under his sixteen wheels, or fall in his path in the confusion; also it is important that the car should be pulled straight, for Jaganath is so holy that he cannot be moved backwards, even an inch. If he should slant across the square and butt against a house, then the house must come down. He may bring ruin as well as redemption in his path.

Pilgrims fight and cluster round the ropes. At the blast of a whistle, the human horses pull, and the traces stretch and stretch, like pieces of elastic. The cottage shudders and seems about to tip forward, then its wheels revolve.

Jaganath has begun his immemorial journey.

A group of priests are dancing on the platform above the yellow coachman, gesticulating and foaming at the mouth whilst the multitude prostrates itself in adoration, or throws showers of marigold and jasmine and money upon the holy car. All over it, men, women and children are clinging and crying and trampling and fainting; for Jaganath gives fertility to the barren, heart's ease to the widow, sons and kine to the householder. The sight of him is bliss unimaginable. He is Lord of the oldest living faith.

Slowly, slowly through his worshippers Jaganath

goes forward, on such a tide of faith and ecstasy as I may never again witness.

Near by, a temple elephant, with the eye of Siva drawn upon his gilded forehead, is watching his hundredth procession. Pilgrims salute him, touching his trappings of cloth-of-gold and then their own foreheads. They give him money, putting annas and even rupees into his trunk : he swings the coins up lazily to a mahout who is almost as *blasé* as himself. Not quite, however, for his master has only seen the show fifty times.

The elephant sways on his soft feet and blinks his small eyes, but not cynically. He seems to be wondering, as indeed I wonder also, why these people, whose *rishis* rejected idolatry several thousand years ago, still bow down to Jaganath.

Neither he nor I can tell. Hindu India flows by us, seething, inscrutable, ecstatic, withdrawn into her sorceries, like Leonardo's women. We can only guess at what lies in her secret heart, and even to guess wisely we must have an imagination that will stretch like the ropes of Jaganath's car.

CHAPTER XVIII

THE TEMPLE OF THE UNDISTRACTED MIND

There came a night in Lucknow when I threw off my mess-dress, medals, Wellington boots, and all my gear as a soldier, as if I could then and there forget these toys and start afresh with new ones. My time as a " bear-leader " was over, and every fibre in me was in revolt against my ghost-like existence as an officer of vanished Bengal Lancers.

The Colonel who commanded our amalgamation made no difficulty about my taking ten days' leave to the hills. There were three dozen officers in our confluent regiments; certainly I could be spared.

Next day, Naim Shah saw me off to Katgodam. He knew this was the beginning of the end of our happy life; and although he disapproved of my cult of strange gods, at the back of his mind he held to a thought which was too great to be uttered, but not difficult to guess for his eyes roved often to a possession of mine which is the Afridi's god. So I gave him a promise, which I shall not particularise owing to the laws about gun licences.

As I travelled towards the Himalayas, I looked out once more over the great plains, which have seen so many conquerors, and say so little to the unquiet West.

It was "cow-dust hour." Ox-carts creaked slowly to a mud-walled village. Blue buffaloes browsed along in front of a naked pot-bellied baby : black-buck bounded high, as if to see the train better : a procession of peasants trailed out towards a shrine : a peacock preened himself by a bamboo covert : men and beasts were gentle and well content. An infinite serenity lay under all that sky.

And as background to this pervasive peace, stood the Himalayas, white and holy, their summits reaching into an after-glow of crimson. Would it be my work, I wondered, to tell the West a little of what may be discovered there, and how Christ Himself threw the light of His divinity upon the truths that were known in the childhood of the Vedas ? The task was broad and big as these plains I travelled, and my equipment scanty. Would anyone listen to the stammering of a soldier ?

I knew little, then, except by instinct. And to-day I have learned only the extent of my ignorance, but I know that even that is worth recording, for others will take up the tale. There are philosophies in India which the nations need, and my own country most of all, for her destiny is bound up with the peoples who profess them.

I had heard that Bhagawan Sri was at Katgodam, preparing for his annual pilgrimage to the Shaivite shrine of Amarnath, but when I arrived there, I found that he had left the previous evening with two disciples.

Hoping to overtake him while still on the highways of civilisation, I hired a car to drive me up to Naini Tal; and had hardly begun enquiring for him in the rambling outskirts of the bazaar below the lake when I saw his tall, loose-limbed, saffron-robed figure at a sweetmeat stall. He was buying parched-barley for his bitch, who sat up and begged for it.

" I have been longing for this moment," I said, as I clasped his hand. " You seem younger, *guru-ji*, than when I saw you nine whole years ago."

" Age is nothing, Sahib. I am happy, too. We have been expecting you for some time."

" Sivanand is with you ? "

" Sivanand and his wife, Sahib. They were married in Cashmere this spring. We three are going to Amarnath together."

" With me, I hope, and your dog ? "

" Come weal or woe, I will never desert my faithful dog," he answered promptly. " Those were the words of Yudisthira on reaching heaven, and I hope to be able to echo them when my time comes."

"And as to me?"

"I see signs that you have progressed in the Path," he answered. "But the journey is a far one."

"I wish I had progressed, *guru-ji*. But while your disciples have been engaged in worship and meditation, I have only been soldiering, which is a waste of time. Or isn't it?"

"You have passed your years of begging and meditation in a different way from ours, that is all. Tell me of the War."

"How can I talk about it, *guru-ji*, when I have so much to hear from you? Has Sivanand been initiated yet? And who is his wife?"

"You will soon find out, Sahib! You and I have all eternity before us, just as Sivanand and Hastini have all eternity in which to study the mysteries of love and devotion. You remember Hastini—who brought you to me?"

"The girl with the limp?"

"Yes. She has become rich in worldly possessions. But they will tell you their story, and you must tell me yours while we walk to the place where we are staying, over there on the terrace by the single tree. Is that a wound on your right arm?"

"It is only a polo accident, *guru-ji*. The War left no outer marks."

"But it made you suffer? Tell me."

His voice was smooth, but I felt that he commanded. There was a core of steel in that benign body.

As we strolled through the bazaar, and on by a mountain path which led away from the lake and upwards to the charcoal-burner's hut at which they had halted, I spoke easily to him of many things which I found it impossible to say to others, for there was a stillness in his mind which drew me out. He seemed to understand everything, and to understand in three dimensions. When I told him of my walk from Winchester to Twyford, for instance, he gauged both my physical and mental states, and saw beyond them to larger questions.

"It is good to love your country," he said, surprisingly, "for war is a disease which patriotism can cure."

"Yet patriotism may lead to terrible conflicts?"

"It may, but it need not. If it does, it is better so. Last year eight millions of us died by influenza. That also is nothing. Siva must take his toll until men know him for what he is. The worst enemy is not death, but wrong desire. Wars are fevers, mass-perversions of the sexual instinct. They come as a fever does, when disease is present; and do good like a fever. The alternative to a fever, when you are diseased, is death. But it is better not to have the disease or the fever, but to love. It is better if your heart is pure."

"A national as well as a personal Yoga?"

"There is no difference, Sahib. A body whose units are in harmony is at peace with all the world."

"But how can there be peace when conflict is a law of Nature? Nature is ugly, *guru-ji*. She makes the turtles eat the dead in the Ganges, and plans the unpleasant fate of various insects, as well as that of humanity. I know your Siva and his Kali now: I first saw her when I had sunstroke, years ago; and again when I killed a favourite horse; and I saw her gloating in the deserts of Mesopotamia. For these last four years she has been dancing on the body of her husband with her girdle of dead hands and bloody breasts, so that the whole earth trembles."

The *guru's* small bright eyes wrinkled in laughter.

"You have seen much and learned much during these years, Sahib," he said, "but you have not learned to love. And love, you know, is the first as well as the last virtue of the Path."

"Can it be taught?"

"You must first learn indifference, Sahib, for love can only come into stillness. You must make a void and then let love flood in from its infinite source. But Sivanand and Hastini will tell you of these things better than I, for they are studying them. Moreover, I must go down the valley, to bathe before the evening meal."

Not one word would he say as to my discipleship. Our talk plunged about like a restive horse, without advancing in any direction; yet it occurred to me now that we had reached the hut, that perhaps he had been the rider and I the steed, and that I was being guided.

The *cheelas* welcomed us with open arms and cries of " Ram ! Ram ! " While the *guru* gathered his brass vessels for washing and drinking, Sivanand and Hastini spread a blanket for me between themselves, and offered me warm milk. Sivanand was the same as he had been at Agra, except that his ropy locks were brushed and parted in the middle, as a sign, perhaps, that he had received the *diksha*[1] which ended his time of wandering. As to Hastini, she seemed to me to be more tidied and more mundane than I remembered her. She wore the saffron robe of a Yogi, like Sivanand, but hers was of silk, and was adorned with a turquoise necklace. A diamond shone in each ear, setting off the glossy black of her short hair, and her caressing eyes.

She told me that she had inherited six villages near Patna on the death of an uncle, and that the Bhagawan Sri had advised her to settle down and administer her inheritance, but that she had begged first to be allowed to visit an *ashram* kept by the Maharajah of Cashmere, and that there she had met Sivanand ; and she told me also of how Sivanand had led her round the sacred marriage fire, and of the lilies on the Dal Lake, and of the garden of Shalimar, and of devil-dancers, and red-cap lamas, and the glittering icicle of Siva in the cave they were to visit. . . .

[1] Initiation.

She talked without pause, simply and smoothly; while I listened with half my mind, and wondered with the other half whether this was really the girl who had stumbled along with me, almost sullenly, towards the Dasaswamedh Ghat.

"And you"—she asked, having exhausted her news—"are you married, Sahib?"

"No, and I don't expect to be," I answered.

"You don't want to have a son to send your spirit on its last journey! I am sorry, Sahib."

When Bhagawan Sri returned, he said in his dry way that I was right not to undertake the duties of a householder, for I was a seeker after the wisdom of the ages. Domestic bliss was not for the *brahmacharin*. They must instruct me in higher matters, he said, such as the mysteries of Being and Not-being and the methods by which the illumined Self may taste the nectar of Attributeless Brahman.

"But what can we teach him while you are here?" protested Hastini.

"I shall not be here," said the *guru*. "Look at the little Western god, on your left wrist, Sahib, and tell me what it says."

"Five-thirty, *guru-ji*!"

"In two hours it will be nearly sunset. Until the shadows lengthen I shall meditate. I am an old man with nothing to say, but you three are young, and can edify yourselves by discussing the quintessence of the Vedanta."

Hastini clapped her hands.

"I understand, *guru-ji*, for you did the same with me! When you are ready," she explained to me, "he will teach you more in five minutes than we can tell you in five years, but not till then. Meanwhile, what shall we talk about?"

"There are so many things——"

"The Sahib is *stiff*!" said Sivanand suddenly.

"Perhaps he doesn't cry and laugh enough," suggested Hastini. "It must be stifling to wear an English mask."

"As to that," I answered, "you know what it is to be shy yourself, I think."

"Indeed I do," she admitted.

Silence fell between us, and the two watched me curiously.

The *guru*, meanwhile, had spread his antelope skin under the single tree. Completely enfolded in his robe, with back and neck as straight as the fir under which he sat, he looked out with unwinking eyes over the mountains where the Vedas were revealed.

Sivanand stretched himself, and lit a cigarette.

"Have you ever tried to calm your mind, Sahib?"

"Of course."

"And how?"

"By relaxing, and—being calm."

"You cannot control thought by thinking. The lungs are the keys to the treasuries of vision. Let us be practical, and talk of that excellent path to peace."

"By all means. And you shall judge for yourself whether or not I have already taken some steps along the road."

"Show me," said Sivanand.

I showed him the *bhastrika* then, as I had practised it in Turkey, but he told me that I had only been wasting my time.

"You will become more flexible with practice," he said. "Your ribs are like an old cask at present. They should be like young branches. Even your tail-bones should move, and your skin should grow luminous and the vital force should tingle at your finger-tips when the lotuses of your body are fully opened."

"Your words slip through my mind, Sivanand. All I know is that this breathing makes me giddy."

"Your heart was not pure if it made you giddy. The life of the body is the blood. The life of the blood is the Spirit. The life of the Spirit is God. God is Spirit, You cannot know Him through the brain, but through the purified and exalted body. As food is turned by the body into blood, and the seed into life, so by the transmutation of divine energy are ideas born. This is a hard saying, even for the gods, and may only be known through purification and active prayer, including *asana* and *mudra*.[1] You will never understand your Self, or

[1] Posture and exercise.

the Creation of which you are a part, as long as you separate it into pieces. Every attribute of the Universe is in your mind. Every quality of your mind—stiffness, strength, fear, joy—is reflected in your body, somewhere, somehow."

"A child can perform every *asana* with ease," added Hastini, "and many of the *mudras*, but not an adult. The seeds of death begin in the joints, and to free them means pain. I know, for I began Yoga only when I was twenty, after a fever in which I would have died but for Bhagawan Sri, and I had almost to break my ankles in order to acquire the lotus seat. For you it will also be difficult."

"And what shall I gain if I do these things?" I asked.

"The right to breathe," she said solemnly, "and therefore a mind at peace, for, as Sivanand says, the breath and brain are linked. You cannot think deep thoughts with shallow lungs and you cannot absorb *prana*[1] through a poisoned body. Hence the necessary purifications. Bliss really begins with the bowels. The *Tantra Sanhita* has a *dhauti*[2] in which the worshipper stands navel deep in water and draws out his long intestine. That is not possible for you. But you can fill it with a gallon of tepid water. Then you must learn to drink water through the nose and expel it through the

[1] Air, which the Hindus have always held to be something more than a mixture of gases.

[2] Purification.

mouth, and drink it through the mouth and expel it through the nose[1]; and the purification of the heart by vomiting,[2] and the ventilation of the alimentary canal by means of the crow-bill pout."[3]

Then, seeing I was puzzled, she continued :

"These things must be learned from a teacher, as also the postures and exercises which force the evil humours from the joints, and enable the seeker after knowledge to concentrate the currents of his body."

"It seems to me you think too much about the body."

"When its gross elements are vivified, Sahib," she answered, "you will understand, but that can only come with practice."

"I think I had better begin now!"

Hastini was utterly in earnest, and took me at my word.

"Begin, then," she said, "by inhaling the beauty of the world : the individuality that the new-born child proclaims with its first cry : the fragrance of the gardens of Shalimar : or the stuff that God gave to your nostrils to make you a living soul, if you like. It is all the same *prana.* Receive it thankfully and humbly. Do not expect to absorb more of it than you are ready to build with. There is no greater sin than pride, and no greater friend than breath : its inspiration, retention and exhalation is your life, and all life ; through it you shall know the truth of Sivagama's words : 'There is

[1] *Vayut Krama* and *s'it Krama.* [2] *Hrid-dhauti* by *vamana.*
[3] *Vatasara-dhauti* by *Kakini-mudra.*

nothing, O Lotus-faced goddess, beyond the breath.' Sivanand will show you, and you can copy him."

Sivanand made me place one hand at his navel and the other at the small of his back. Then he swelled himself with air and collapsed himself with rhythmic speed, each inhalation seeming like a light hammer-tap. Finally, with breath retained and eyes upturned, he remained still, yet strangely vibrant. Through this hidden energy I drew through him a sense of power, not directly derived from his physical envelope, but coming, perhaps, from all thought in all worlds. I saw distant minds and the souls of the dead, and reached out to them with the fingers of spirit, but grasped only air : I could not enter them.

" Once a *guru* was able to possess himself of the mind and body of a Queen of Benares by this power of *prana*, so that he became the Queen herself," said Sivanand. " But the control of such forces is very difficult. The *bhastrika* is first of all a cleansing breath. Beyond that you need not look. During the inward breath, imagine that you are absorbing some portion of the Cosmic Consciousness. During the outward breath, send your spirit out to the four corners of the earth. And during the holding of the breath, listen attentively to the life within. In that stillness the five illusions fade in the knowledge of Siva, and Reality is seen as a candle in a windless place. The flame is in every heart, but it cannot shine amidst confusions of desire."

Three times I took twenty-one breaths and held my breath.

The first time I felt as if something had caught me by the throat.

The second time I again felt suffocated, but knew that *prana* was mobilising the armies of the blood and forcing its way through the barriers of the body. There was a struggle between opposing forces, a descent into hell, a search of Orpheus for his bride ; then so-called mind asserted its dominion over so-called matter, light replaced darkness and my stimulated blood-stream flooded through every cell. I felt buoyant and calm and intuitively aware.

The third time, a sense of ease and equipoise almost instantly replaced the initial struggle, and with this physical balancing came an apprehension untellable. With my Angel I took wings of wonder and traversed continents and worlds, and seemed to reach the last stars, beyond thinking, where mind is not, and where that nothing out of which came something seems almost clutchable.

" If you practise this restraint three times a day for six months at regular hours," said Sivanand, " you may begin to obtain results."

" Results ? "

" Sounds : they will be but your own blood in your arteries. Sights : images in your own retina if you care to separate them from other illusions. Sensations : the quivering of *Kundalini* in the spine, if you so imagine it. But if I tell you what to expect, what you expect will come to pass, but not in its natural order. You must have confidence. Open your heart and lungs to the source of life and *prana* will work for you. Remember that the purpose of all *pranayama*—and this is a truth on which you must ponder—is to make the breath come slowly and slowly. When its inspiration and expiration are exactly balanced, you will have peace of mind, whether you know it or not."

Bhagawan Sri, I remembered, had told me the same at Benares. What was he doing now, I wondered, so aloof and still?

An hour and a half had passed, and still he remained immobile, unseeing, as if carved against a red sky. Sivanand guessed my thought.

"We could not disturb him, even if we would, Sahib, for he is rapt. But let us go to him, for he would not have meditated like this in the open unless he had desired you to see him."

We went to the place where he sat, followed by the terrier, growling.

"Touch him," said Sivanand, "and you will see that he is cold. He is with his *shakti*, in the isolation of bliss. He has drawn *Kundalini* upwards so that all life has left his body except in one place. The thousand-petalled jewel of the lotus glows. There only his life burns in one fiery point."

I hesitated, but the *cheelas* made me put my hand on his ankles and his neck. They were icy-cold. His eyes were turned upwards into his skull. He did not seem to breathe. To all intents and purposes he was dead, except that the extreme top of his head was hot.

"Do not be alarmed, Sahib," said Hastini. "He can recall *Kundalini* at will."

"You are sure that he can come back?"

"He will bring *Kundalini* down at nightfall," said Hastini. "Come, Sahib, you are cold."

She drew her arm through mine, and we returned to the hut. The glow of her body warmed me through and through.

A curious comprehension seemed to link us, but whatever this understanding was, she was its mistress as she was its begetter: she could make me burn or freeze, but I did not feel that I had any effect on her.

She began to speak of that serpent-lore of the Tantriks which is at once so mystical and so material that it baffles the Western mind.

"The goddess is more subtle than the fibre of the lotus," she said, "and lies asleep at the base of the spine, curled three-and-a-half times round Herself, closing with Her body the door of Brahman. Sometimes She awakes of Her own volition, which you call falling in love. Falling in love! Yes, like slipping on a mango skin. The right way to arouse Her is through breathing. Then you do not fall, but rise into love. Then She uncoils Herself, and raises Her head, and enters the royal road of the spine, piercing the mystic centres, until She reaches the brain. These things are not to be understood in a day. When She reaches the thousand-petalled jewel of the lotus, then the Sun at the navel meets the Moon at the throat, and you taste Her nectar, and know that She is Life, and that Life is God."

Hastini held me as if I had been entranced. I could not take my eyes from hers : they were my gates of pearl.

One can, if one will, describe what happens when four hands meet. One can, if one will, describe the sudden understanding between a man and woman, the conflagrant moment when two Selves come into the sunlight of unity, knowing each other. But there are moments stranger still, which no tongue can tell, or pen write, when nothing happens on the physical plane, unless the eyes between themselves spin some etheric web in which something dances, like the sex-chromosomes in the womb. It is not in the body alone that a child is born. Every woman carries within her another seed : she is the begetter of more than bodies. That which was born between Hastini and I that night still lives, and can therefore reproduce its kind, but what and where it is I cannot say.

*** *** *** ***

When the *guru* returned, he joined in our conversation as if he had never left us. I did ask him about his trance, for the talk still ran on the mysteries of love and devotion, and Bhagawan Sri was disposed to listen to his *cheelas*. " Sivanand and I have renounced even the Veda." Hastini was saying: " We are crossing the ocean of Maya, and we do not know what we shall find on its farther shore. But after all this is the play-time of the spirit that cannot always live in one room, nor always fix its thoughts on eternity."

" The wife and the mother is the sole and sacred path," said Bhagawan Sri, quoting a text. " In her you shall be born again."

Hastini considered this a moment, and added a saying of Bhartihari's :

" ' The true object of love is the union of the hearts of the participants. When that is not accomplished, the mating might be that of two corpses.' "

" Through breathing you shall come to *Laya-siddhi*," said Bhagawan Sri, " as through walking you reach a place of pilgrimage. Sivanand will find Her who is his hidden half, and you, Hastini, Him. The true knowledge of Being comes out of the masculine awakening in woman, and the feminine in man, which is manifested on the earth-plane as sexual union. In that super-sensual bliss the rock of egoism is riven, and the two become One, and Very God."

" And then, after a long time," said Sivanand, " when we see the children of our children, we shall abandon all food taken in towns and take refuge in a lonely forest. And so we shall have escaped from the net of desire, although still together, and Siva shall be seen by us in his true aspect."

"Instead of as Kali," I said, "who dances upon the body of her husband?"

"Yes, Sahib, instead of in the *mayik* form necessary for creation. Every instant upon this earth there is a great out-pouring of fertility. Every second a new-born child is somewhere crying, and somewhere another soul is leaving the skull it inhabits. These changes pertain to *maya*; their perception is the higher wisdom. There are a million lives in Sivanand, waiting to meet Hastini's. Their wills shall choose them, by a knowledge and control of their dual natures which is the microcosm of the world-process between Siva and his *shakti*."

Again I suspected, but I think now wrongly, that Bhagawan Sri was not being as explicit as he might have been.

We ate a few mangoes and drank a little milk. We looked up to the stars, and warmed ourselves at our fire. Sivanand smoked incessantly.

"I have found clues, *guru-ji*, to some of the things which I have been seeking," I said at last, "but there is one of my questions which you have avoided. To-morrow I shall know the answer; so why not tell me now whether I may come to Amarnath?"

The *guru* took a piece of biscuit and showed it to his

terrier, who jumped round him expectantly. When he tossed it up, she caught it in mid-air.

"Look at that for concentration!" he said. "That is the quality of *ekagrata*, the faculty of sinking the mind in space, as a lover into the arms of his adored."

"You will not take me?"

"The bee buzzes when it is outside the flower," said Bhagawan Sri, "but within the chalice it drinks honey silently. In the West you may find a *guru* who knows the skilful management of your times and values, to lead you to the threshold of the temple of the undistracted mind."

I swallowed my disappointment. In the light of the embers over which we crouched, I could see Hastini's eyes, narrowed, observant, like a line of black bees in a summer sky.

We talked far into the night, of many things of both East and West; and I knew that I was receiving a lesson in that virtue of the Path which complements love.

We spoke of the teachings of Christianity in regard to death (the *guru* considered that we sometimes relinquished this life with an unseemly struggle); and of the connexion between modern mathematics and the word *iva*—relativity—so constantly appearing in the Vedas; and again of breathings such as the *brahmarai*,[1] and the *sitali*,[2] and the one-four-two rhythm,

[1] A droning sound. [2] A serpent-hiss.

by which the mind may pass behind the lights and shadows of the phenomenal world.

" How may the knower cut the knot of appearances with a knife of grey pulp ? " said Sivanand. " A knock against the hard facts of existence may blunt the brain : too much sleep may rust it : too little sleep may make it as brittle as a dry twig. Then snap—you cannot know Reality until your next incarnation ! "

Presently I lay down, telling myself I could listen better like that.

" Your civilisation has done marvellous things," he continued, sucking at the cup of his hands in which a cigarette burned, so that he drew in lungfuls of mixed smoke and air. " You have almost conquered the earth. With your telescopes and trains and battleships you can move and control almost everything, except your thoughts, and the food in your bowels. . . . You look outwards too much. Our methods are more reasonable. We do not bother about engines. The *shakti-nadi* is a more important machine."

I rose, startled. Sivanand was still speaking, but in another tone.

" As the dew is dried by the morning light," he was saying, " so are the sins of mankind dispersed by the glories of Himalaya."

Then Hastini capped him with : "He who has seen Himalaya is greater than he who has performed all the worships of Kashi."

Hours had passed, and although it was not yet dawn, its foreglow had already lit three hundred miles of snow before me, remote, and plumed with storms that never cease ; yet in appearance so close and so quiet that it seemed to me that I might stroll there in an hour or two, and bask in a white peace.

The three now sat silent, with the old bitch at my *guru's* feet, looking over those titanic masses that have given India her fertility and her faith. In the increasing light, the clouds above them took the shape of beasts. A dragon pounced on the mountains of Nepal, a lizard with eyes of flame devoured a fly upon Nanda Devi, a sprawling giantess stretched her length from Trisul to Diwalghiri and searched the valleys with a luminous rapier.

Surya had begun the skyey chase that never ends. For all his pains he can do no more than touch the hem of the twilight maid, and gather the roses of morning that she scatters. Yet it is for her that the world is lit. But for her, flowers would not open, nor man walk the earth. But for her darkness, there would be no light.

The old mountains looked indulgently on the five of us who faced the shrines of Aryavarta. Buddhas and birds and butterflies and trees were one to them. The world was still young, and full of a blossoming and a fluttering and a search for things unfindable.

The sun lit up the yellow robes of my friends, and their lips moved, but I heard no sound, for the Gayatri is very sacred :

OM TAT SAVITUR VARENYAM BHARGO DEVASYA DIMOHI DHIYO YO NAH PRACHODAYAT OM.

O face of the True Sun, now hidden by a disc of gold, may we know Thy Reality, and do our whole duty on our journey to Thy Light.[1]

" *Guru-ji*, when may I say that prayer ? "

" Soon or late you will be one of us, for there is that within a man which is stronger than any outer circumstance. When you have learned more of the breath which is a reflex of the Great Breath, you will notice the tricks time plays on man, and know that it is not within the frame of our measurements."

" In this dawn I am aware of that ! "

" You have begun to be aware of love. But mortal mind cannot know its heights and depths. In the Upanishads it is written that in the beginning nor time nor change, nor speech, nor shape, nor Aught, nor

[1] This is what I understand the Gayatri to mean : the literal translation is " Let us contemplate that glorious Light of the divine Savitur : may He inspire our minds."

Naught, existed. Love came to this emptiness as the in-drawn breath of cosmos, and out of it the worlds were made. Nature and Will were formed then and both are bound by Love, so that the three are one. Every religion in the world says this, and I have studied them all ! "

The words rang true. In his mind, so resilient and so sane, were faiths flooded over by the sands of Atlantis and Chaldea ; the Vaishna trident and the Shaivite eye were there ; the seal of twi-sexed Hermes, the vulture cap of Isis, the serpent-circled rod, the Crescent and the Cross. And as all colours mingle and merge in sunlight, so in him the blending of these beliefs showed forth love.

THE END

APPENDIX

APPENDIX

The word Yoga comes from root *yug*, meaning to join: it signifies the union of the body of the disciple with the visible world, and of his spirit with cosmic consciousness. Further, Yoga has the sense of a yoke, or discipline, which the student must undergo in order to reach happiness and heaven.

Yoga, as I know it, is monistic. "All that exists is one, though sages call it by different names." Many centuries after these Vedic words were written St. Athanasius was made responsible for the idea that: "the reasonable soul and flesh is one man. One, not by conversion of the God-head into flesh; but by taking of the manhood into God; one altogether, not by confusion of substance: but by unity of person."

There is no notion in Yoga, as I know it, of a divinity disjunct from the Self, no doctrine of a Creator ruling His Universe from an outside heaven. Such a possibility may be admitted or implied in some Hindu scriptures, but my *guru*, at any rate, concerned himself entirely with Man and his Becoming.

Yoga is the study of You.

The body of the Yogi is the universe. It is not, however, either so material or so metaphysical a body as is commonly believed; but the whole subject is so enmeshed in prejudice, misunderstanding, and unfamiliar Sanskrit terms that I despair of condensing into a few thousand words what Arthur Avalon and Professor Radha Krishnan have discussed brilliantly—in many volumes.

I take courage, however, from the fact that the knowledge of the Vedas is beginning to spread in Europe. "In the whole world there is no study so beneficial or so elevating," said Schopenhauer, adding that "the Vedas have been the solace of my life: they will be the solace of my death." On this Max Müller observed that "if the words of Schopenhauer required any endorsement from me I would willingly give it as the result of my own experiences during a long life devoted to the study of many philosophies and many religions. If by philosophy is meant a preparation for a happy death, I know no preparation better than the philosophy of the Vedas. The early Indians possessed a knowledge of the true God. All their writings are replete with sentiments and expressions that are noble, clear and severely grand. Not to know what the Vedas have already done in illuminating the darkest passages of the human mind—of that mind on which we ourselves are feeding and living—is a misfortune." Two modern authorities (Sir John Woodroffe and M. Maeterlinck) support these statements. The former, in *The World as Power-Reality*, claims that "an examination of Indian Vedic doctrine shows that it is, in important respects, in conformity with the most advanced scientific and philosophic thought of the West, and that when this is not so, it is science which will go to the Vedanta and not the reverse"; while M. Maeterlinck, in *La Grande Féerie*, writing of the problems of time and space, says: "Seule, à l'origine des âges, l'antique religion de l'Inde eut l'intuition de ces gigantesques et insolubles problèmes. Elle regardait l'univers en mouvement comme une illusion qui apparait ou disparait selon un rhythme sans fin que scandent le sommeil et le reveil de la Cause Eternelle. . . . N'est-ce pas dans cette voie que marche notre science?"

But Hindu philosophy will require many more libraries and expositors—say another thousand man-years of work—before it is rightly valued in the West. A system whose scriptures number five hundred volumes and go back five thousand years cannot be understood in a day, or even in a generation. To sift and refine, to analyse and compare, will be a labour in which the exact scholarship of Europe and America may co-operate with the intuitive feeling-realisation of the race to whom the Vedas belong. Already the University of Oxford has published some forty translations of Sanskrit texts. Harvard has published twenty-six texts, and Johns Hopkins the whole of the Atharva Veda, but there are many more books that await translation, and even discovery, for some of the Tantrik scriptures have been hidden away.

Further, there is an immense exegesis in Sanskrit, German, French and English ; and, incomparably more important than all else, there still exists a living tradition of Vedic culture by the banks of the Ganges. The Brahmins of to-day, like their ancestors, have a great appetite for abstractions : they have always discussed everything and tried everything of which man has ever thought. In a material sense this has perhaps been their undoing, but it has also been a source of inner strength. No other race has delved so deep into the Unconscious. And no other race has survived so long in racial purity. Theirs is the most ancient civilisation on earth. Benares was a venerable town when London and Paris were villages. Down the centuries the Brahmins have carried the torch of the Vedas above the heads of the crowd, and they are rightly proud of the light it has given the world.

But with Hindu philosophy as a whole I am only indirectly concerned. I have no knowledge of the meditational environments of the *ashrams* and monasteries of Asia. There is only one branch of Yoga which I have experienced in my bones and breathing, and that a very practical one, which would be well adapted to meet the increasing nervous strain of modern life.

The Hindus have never held that matter is some inert outside substance. It is a commonplace with them that the body is an aspect of the mind. God is life. Life is God. Yoga is an orderly and objective process of self-realisation ; the handmaid of religion, not a religion in itself. It has nothing to do with mystery and Mahatmas.

Moreover, there is more than one Yoga. Here are six, which I have set down as a concession to our Western love for classification :

1. *Mantra Yoga*, or the science of vibrations ;

2. *Gnana Yoga*, in which the intellect is invoked to obtain a knowledge of heaven ;

3. *Bhakti Yoga*, where the disciple finds " paradise here in this body pent " by means of love and devotion ;

4. *Karma Yoga*, which is the philosophy of work and the attainment of happiness through action ;

5. *Raja Yoga*, which aims at a synthesis *Gnana*, *Karma* and *Bhakti* Yoga by service and self-sacrifice in the management of worldly affairs ;

And 6. *Hatha* or *Gathastha Yoga*, with which I have been chiefly concerned, and which seeks in its early stages to awaken the sleeping serpent of *Kundalini*, or vitality, by a physiological psychology.

But there is no real dividing line between these Yogas nor between the eight stages (corresponding to the Buddhist's " noble eight-fold path ") into which every one of them is divided. These stages are :

1. Right thought, or *yama-niyama*, meaning literally "death-not death." The pundit at Delhi gave me a list of these preliminary virtues, which includes the moralities of all religions.

2. *Asana*, or right positions. These relate to the balance and posture of the body. Buddha, for instance, is generally represented with his right foot on his left thigh and his left foot on his right, in what is known as the lotus seat, which has as definite an effect on the mind as has the Christian *asana* of kneeling in prayer.

3. *Mudra* consists of exercises and gestures, including the *dhauties*, or purifications, or baptisms.

4. *Pranayama* is the study of the various rhythms of breathing. It cannot be undertaken until both mind and body have been rendered supple and pure by previous exercises.

The four succeeding stages are : 5. *Pratyahara*, 6. *Dharana*, 7. *Dhyana*, and 8. *Samadhi*. These steps are described at great length in some English works on Yoga, but the true teaching never will and never can be put in print, being personal and infinitely flexible. All that is written in Sanskrit concerning it is in the nature of notes or outlines to enable the *guru* to pass on the teaching to his *cheela* in the accustomed order. Roughly, *pratyahara* is nerve control ; *dharana*, mind control ; *dhyana*, meditation ; *samadhi*, bliss, isolation, emancipation, ecstasy. The Jesuits, whose exercises Loyola may have borrowed from Moorish mysticism, possess the nearest approach to *dhyana* in the West.

Before the fourth stage can be entered upon (*pranayama*) three baptisms are necessary ; by water, fire and the Holy Ghost. Baptism by water is of the skin, teeth, nasal passages and lower bowel. Purification by fire is concerned with control of the digestive system—for an active metabolism is considered in Yoga as a function of purity. Finally the sloughing of the shell of egoism, the preparation of the mind for the illumination of the Spirit, is a combination of exercises for the cerebro-spinal and sympathetic nervous systems together with an individual course of character-training under the *guru*. Hot baths and white linen will not of themselves make us clean ; nor sexual repressions. The Eastern purity is more thorough than ours, and insists on an elimination of poisons of the intestinal tract, a proper digestion of food, and a riddance of the lumber of thwarted will and unsatisfied desire that hamper the brain.

Here in the West we make an exact science of medicine and are inclined to consider religion as something rather esoteric ; the Brahmins, on the contrary, see in our body a mystical microcosm of the Universe, and in ideas about God only a formal and rather sterile intellectual exercise.

A balance between these views would certainly contribute to the advancement of knowledge and be of benefit to both races. The Hindus, as I think they would themselves admit, should come closer to certain practical realities ; as to ourselves, if we studied the mystical phenomena of India, we might well discover facts of importance not only to Harley Street, but to Christendom.

I am a Christian myself, and it seems to me clear that Christ based his teaching on a tradition existing in His time and country, and that that tradition originally came from India, and is still being followed there, passing from father to son, from *guru* to *cheela*, with some accretions and superstitions perhaps, yet still one of the most ancient of languages " in which men have spoken of their God."

Consider, for instance, the healing miracles of Christ from the standpoint of the aphorisms of Patanjali. In the vivid and mysterious 11th chapter of the Gospel according to St. John, the disciple whom Jesus loved would appear to have been prepared for an ancient exercise, no doubt practised by the Essenes of that time as it is by the Copts to-day, and known in India as the *Kali-mudra*.[1]

This *Kali-mudra* is a self-induced trance which is only entered into by the aptest pupils of a great teacher, and then only after preparation and purification, for it is dangerous, and success in it is proof that the student can transcend the limitations of time in his own flesh. Quite properly, such powers were kept secret in past ages. Even to-day they are not for the crowd, but if they do exist (and I know that they are still being practised) then I think that knowledge of them would elucidate certain incidents in the life of the Founder of our Faith.

There is nothing in the following " reconstruction " of the story of Lazarus that need strain our sense of probability.

First, then, let us assume, as we surely may, that the mysteries of the Kingdom of Heaven were given to

[1] Literally, " death-gesture."

some and not to others of those whom Christ taught. Between Jesus and the Little Eleazer (Lazarus is an affectionate diminutive ; moreover he was unmarried, which again points to discipleship) there existed some special bond which may well have been that of master to initiate.

Lazarus stopped breathing. His heart-beat could not be felt. Naturally his sisters thought that he was dead and sent word to Jesus, their friend.

What did Jesus do ? Hurry to the house that had so often sheltered Him and help the boy to whom He had given His divine love ? On the contrary, He said that the sickness was " not unto death, but for the glory of God "—words which seem to indicate that Lazarus was undergoing a step in his training which the Master did not wish to interrupt.

The disciples come to the Master and say that if Lazarus is only asleep " he will do well." There is no reason, they add, to risk the danger of a journey into Judea.

Two days pass. Lazarus has not yet awakened from his trance and is now in danger.

Then Jesus says to his disciples plainly, " Lazarus is dead."

To all intents and purposes Lazarus is dead, for unless the Master raises him, the ordeal will end in tragedy. First Jesus says that the sleep is not unto death and two days later that the sleeper is dead : how better are we to account for the apparent contradiction in Christ's words than by the hypothesis that Lazarus has been in a trance ? No other explanation, it seems to me, will square with all the facts given in the Fourth Gospel.

Jesus comes to Bethany and finds that His disciple has been in the grave for four days. Martha says, " Lord, if Thou hadst been here my brother had not died." True, Lazarus would not have died. But each soul must go out alone to meet its God : the divine arms can only help it after it has tried to walk.

The terrible moment of His tears and groaning as He

draws near the tomb is now understandable (indeed it is suffused with new light) if we accept this theory. The one being who could have understood the hidden side of His teaching and might therefore have given Him a human sympathy, has been unable, through bodily weakness, to carry the burden of the knowledge given. Amongst these folk Jesus feels himself surrounded by love, but not by comprehension. Lazarus knew a little more than they, but less than He had hoped. A friend has failed him, not for the first or last time.

When the stone is about to be removed, Martha says that the body will stink. So it would have in that climate ; but Yogis have been known to remain as long as forty days in ***Kali-mudra***.

They take away the stone. Jesus lifts up His eyes and says : " Father, I thank Thee that Thou hast heard Me." Then he calls Lazarus in a loud voice (or a " piercing " voice, for the dearly-loved voice of the Master must reach a numbed consciousness) and the soul of the disciple is brought back from the borderland where it hovers.

Christ speaks and there is life.